School

BASED ON THE PBS SERIES

School: The Story of American Public Education

PRODUCED BY SARAH MONDALE AND SARAH B. PATTON,
DIRECTED BY SARAH MONDALE, EDITED BY
MARIAN SEARS HUNTER, AND WRITTEN
BY SHEILA CURRAN BERNARD

School

THE STORY OF

American Public Education

Foreword by Meryl Streep

INTRODUCTION BY DAVID TYACK

WITH JAMES D. ANDERSON, LARRY CUBAN,
CARL F. KAESTLE, AND DIANE RAVITCH

NARRATIVE BY SHEILA CURRAN BERNARD
AND SARAH MONDALE

Edited by Sarah Mondale and Sarah B. Patton

BEACON PRESS BOSTON

BEACON PRESS
25 Beacon Street
Boston, Massachusetts 02108-2892
www.beacon.org

Beacon Press books are published under the auspices of
the Unitarian Universalist Association of Congregations.

Printed in the United States of America

13 12 11 10   13 12 11

This book is printed on acid-free paper that meets the uncoated paper
ANSI / NISO specifications for permanence as revised in 1992.

Design and composition by Wilsted & Taylor Publishing Services

Library of Congress Cataloging-in-Publication Data
School, the story of American public education / edited by Sarah Mondale and
Sarah B. Patton ; introduction by David Tyack, with James D. Anderson . . . [et al.] ;
narrative by Sheila Curran Bernard and Sarah Mondale ; foreword by Meryl Streep.
p. cm.
Based on the PBS series "School, the story of American public education,"
produced and directed by Sarah Mondale and Sarah Patton.
Includes bibliographical references and index.
ISBN 978-0-8070-4220-5 (cloth)
ISBN 978-0-8070-4221-2 (pbk.)
1. Education—United States—History. 2. Public schools—
United States—History. I. Mondale, Sarah. II. Patton, Sarah B.
III. School, the story of American public education (Television program).
LA212 .S353 2001
370´.973—dc21   2001002714

If it's a school day, during school hours, one-fifth of the total American population consists of public school students K through 12. One in five Americans. And if you count teachers and administrators you are probably going to get pretty close to one-quarter of the population of the country at any given time on a weekday sitting in a public school building.

NICHOLAS LEMANN

Contents

Foreword

When we think about our days in school, we often recall a particular teacher who made the most difference in our lives. For me, it was my music teacher, Claire Callahan. I was in high school and thought she was inconceivably old—something like twenty-four. She was a guitar student of Andrés Segovia. She didn't have enough money for her lessons, so she came to my suburban school in New Jersey and taught music. She was absolutely amazing.

Teachers perform major miracles in America, daily. My interest in public education comes from the respect I have for what teachers do and is very personal. My brother teaches in a New York City public high school, and I'm really proud of him. He has made me aware of the issues that our teachers face, a lot of them having to do with the lack of attention that they receive and their low salaries. I went to public schools in New Jersey as a child and have sent my children to public and private schools on over four continents and two coasts. They've been in every kind of school you can imagine—in Africa, England, Australia, Texas, California, New York, and Connecticut.

Once I became a parent, it confounded me that the school in my district in

Connecticut was always underfunded. First we couldn't get uniforms for our band. Then we couldn't get instruments. Then, well, perhaps we wouldn't have a music program at all. And the school needed a lot of money that was raised, and contributed, by parents. I thought back to when I was growing up. In our school we had had a band. We had had an enormous hot lunch served in the cafeteria. We had had a new school with an auditorium where plays were staged. When I sent my kids to public school, I had to pack lunch for them. My kids held plays not in an auditorium, but in the gym. Why is this? Why, after World War II when everybody was coming out of the army and didn't have a lot of money, a time when everyone on my street lived in small houses, did we have fabulous schools? Somehow, when I was growing up, we were able to have a wonderful music teacher. And a fantastic art department. And a drama department in which I got my start, as Marian the Librarian in *The Music Man,* and for which I'm very grateful.

I wonder at the reasons behind the differences in public schools then and now. An evident one is that money was spent on public schools after the war because they were deemed important. Another reason is that at that time, many very bright women had no other place to put their intelligence and ambition except in the school system. Those women now are in law school; they are doctors; they have other kinds of lives that give them other advantages, including better pay. We've lost some great teachers. To keep this from continuing to happen, we need to pay more to people who teach. I think that if we were to make the positions in inner-city schools more valuable, we would immediately draw people to teach there.

We've reached a controversial moment in the history of public education, a time when we must pay attention to our schools and invest in the specific school systems that need help. This book takes a historical look at public education while keeping an eye on the present. It teaches us that all the questions we ask about public education today have been considered at some point before. And it reminds us that public education for all Americans is relatively new, and something we cannot afford to take for granted.

MERYL STREEP
March 12, 2001

Foreword

School

Introduction

Schools are the most familiar of all civic institutions. You find them in city slums and leafy suburbs, Appalachian valleys and mining towns high in the Rockies. If you fly over the prairies that stretch endlessly across the middle of the United States, you see below you a patchwork of the farms and municipalities neatly laid out in townships, each composed of thirty-six sections. More than two centuries ago the federal government laid out these civic checkerboards and pledged that the inhabitants of the western territories could use the revenue generated from the sixteenth section of each township to support education. The public ("common") schools supported by these land grants were emblems of a common citizenship across the new nation and even newer western states, but they were also civic centers of their local communities in long-established towns as well as frontier settlements.

One article of faith among the founding fathers was that a republic could survive only if its citizens were educated. School has continued to shape the core of our national identity. "The free common school system," Adlai Stevenson once said, is "the most American thing about America."

Early in the nineteenth century, Thomas Jefferson argued that locally con-

1

trolled public schools were key democratic institutions in two ways. By teaching correct political principles to the young, they could nurture virtuous citizens. Equally important, local control gave adult citizens a chance to exercise self-rule. In the twentieth century, John Dewey voiced a similar commitment to education in democracy through an emphasis on political socialization and wise collective choices. For these philosophers of democracy, education was a common good, not simply an individual consumer good.

But achieving a sense of common purpose has never been easy. For two centuries, public school districts have been political arenas in which citizens have contended with one another. In a society as socially diverse as the United States, controversies about purposes and practices in public schooling are hardly surprising. Such policy debates express both hopes and fears about the nation. When citizens deliberate about the education of the young, they are also debating the shape of the future for the whole nation.

Talk about schooling has been part of a larger attempt to define what historian Thomas Bender calls "the public culture." He says that the struggle of groups for "legitimacy and justice" has created and recreated this public culture and established "our common life as a people and as a nation." It is essential, he adds, to understand "why some groups and some values have been so much—or so little—represented in public life and in mainstream culture and schooling at any given moment in our history."

To some people, the notion of common values taught in a common school seems outdated or naive at this time in history. Today, some critics deride "government schools" as inefficient, bureaucratic, and coercive. Some say that Americans are so different that shared civic values are impossible. Ethnic and racial groups attack bias in traditional accounts of American history, and debates over what should be a canon of standard knowledge reverberate in Congress and state capitals as well as the groves of academe.

By many accounts, public schools are in trouble today. Grim stories appear daily in the media about violence, high dropout rates, and low test scores. Beyond such immediate concerns lies an uneasiness about purpose, a sense that we have lost our way. As the larger purposes that once gave resonance to public education have become muted, constituencies that at one time supported public education have become splintered and confused about what to do.

Policy talk about education has always contained plenty of hype and alarm —the hellfire-and-damnation sermon followed by the certain solution. Recent talk may set a record for moving without missing a beat from tales of catastrophe to promises of revolutionary reform.

School does not gloss over the recent crisis of confidence or the array of practical problems in education. But it suggests that the recent maelstrom of criticism and defense of public schooling has left little space for deliberation about what unites as well as divides citizens, what part broad civic goals have played within a pluralistic society, what features of the common school are worth preserving, and how education has (and has not) adapted to the remarkable pluralism of the American population.

Perhaps one reason many Americans feel that we have lost our way in education is that we have forgotten where we have been. Reformers often say that they don't want to look backwards, arguing that amnesia is a virtue when it comes to reinventing education. The problem with that stance is that it is impossible. Everyone uses some sense of the past in everyday life, and leaders cannot escape thinking in time. The real question is whether the histories we all use in decision making enrich and ground our understanding of the choices we face.

History does not proffer simple lessons. If it did, historians would probably not disagree so much with each other. But study of the past can provide context for decisions and images of possibility and constraint.

The story that *School* tells is complex and controversial and open-ended, in keeping with the aspirations, fears, achievements, and failures of citizens and educators, past and present. It explores how Americans have sought to shape their society through public education. It invites readers to step back from today's formulations of problems and solutions, to think about where we have been and where we might go.

Foreign observers of American society during the century following independence often commented on how much U.S. citizens distrusted government at a distance, whether that of King George III or spendthrift state legislatures. Voters wanted to keep legislators on a short leash and kept rewriting their state constitutions to weaken government. Partly because of this deep-rooted distrust of government, Americans have, over the years, been slow to provide social and health services through public agencies (a fact well known to proponents of medical coverage for all citizens today).

Thus in the middle of the nineteenth century, the advocates of public education realized that they had a job to do. They faced rugged competition from a host of private schools of many varieties. Families with resources had many choices in the educational marketplace—some public, some private, some charitable and some for profit, some sectarian and some secular. The results of this miscellaneous schooling were impressive: well before the majority of children attended public schools, both attendance in school and literacy rates were quite high. By 1890, public schools became dominant and enrolled about nine in ten pupils.

Government-distrusting, tax-pinching, independent Americans might well have chosen to continue to rely on this diverse collection of schools to educate their children. They did not. Instead, they chose, collectively and decisively, to establish and sustain the world's most universal and popular system of education.

In doing so, they stayed close to their roots and formed the most decentralized system of school governance in the world. They controlled and financed schools locally. Public education would not have thrived without this self-rule. It enabled citizens to keep a close eye on their schools and to resolve issues by local majority rule. American school board members constituted the largest group of public officials in the world during the late nineteenth century. They outnumbered teachers in a number of rural states.

But considering local self-rule leads to a puzzle: why was this grassroots schooling so similar, at least across the North, when no central ministry of education set standards and enforced regulations? Adam Smith claimed that the "invisible hand" of the market worked more effectively than a directive government. In the United States, it was a common set of political and social values that helped to produce similar common schools scattered across the nation. Shared beliefs encouraged people to build institutions, and over time citizens came to believe that schooling was a public good essential to the health of the nation. Individuals did benefit from schooling, yes, but even more important, civic society depended on instilling common values.

But what were these values to be? An inclination to compete lay deep in the American grain. Throughout the nineteenth century, churches vied with each other for souls and members; how could they agree on common principles? The nineteenth century was also a time of lusty contest between the political parties; they delighted in puncturing the claims and pretenses of the opposition. And raw conflict—red in tooth and claw—marked much of the economic history of the time. So why did Americans hope that they could agree about the moral and civic lessons that schools should teach when they clashed so vigorously in most other arenas?

Horace Mann, the great nineteenth-century school reformer, and thousands of other state and local leaders had a plan. Surely, they said, the warring religious groups could call a truce at the door of the common school for the sake of the children and the nation. They developed an argument that they thought was self-evident: the main purpose of public education is to develop good character; character is based on religion; religion is based on the central teachings of the Bible; therefore, moral education should be based on reading the Bible without sectarian comment. This "nonsectarian" religion of consensus appealed to the Protestant mainstream that supplied most of the leadership of public education. Catholics clearly saw that this set of propositions did not match their doctrine. In response, they decided to challenge the common school by creating their own schools.

Hand in hand with this doctrine of nonsectarian moral teaching was the claim that political education could be nonpartisan. In this theory, the common school should teach only those pure republican principles and practices that united Americans. This pedagogy of patriotism is most obvious in American history textbooks that glorified the founding fathers. The compilers of the famous McGuffey readers promised that they contained no sectarian or partisan accounts and included solely those values that everyone subscribed to (or should subscribe to). There was a huge market for such a political and religious common denominator: the McGuffey readers racked up sales of over 122 million copies.

The creation of the common school, with its grassroots governance and consensual curriculum, was one of the triumphs of nineteenth-century reform. Fueled by a powerful republican ideology and aspiring to create universal education, the common school movement appealed to millennial hope and fear. But by the turn of the twentieth century, reformers grew dissatisfied with local self-rule and a shared curriculum.

Introduction

5

Once again, the country came to a turning point in the development of its system of education, as leaders redefined democracy in the new urban and industrial society of the early twentieth century. Their vision of democracy in the twentieth century exalted experts and denigrated widespread lay participation.

Local control by elected school committees had set a democratic stamp on public education, but policy elites at the turn of the twentieth century complained that the efforts of rural school trustees fell short. They gave local citizens just what they wanted: schooling that was cheap, that reflected local notions of useful learning, and that gave employment to local teachers who fit in well with the community. One leader denounced local control by district trustees as "democracy gone to seed." How could penny-pinching and provincial rural trustees prepare youth for the twentieth century?

Elite reformers also believed that the leadership in urban districts was poor. They felt that the central urban school committees were far too large and delegated decisions to subcommittees of trustees rather than to the experts. They felt that too many of the wrong people ran things, and they pointed especially to corrupt machine politicians and to immigrants who wanted the schools to respect their cultures and to hire their daughters. How could urban schools become efficient and professional, how could they "Americanize" immigrants, with all these foxes in the chicken coops? Worse, many cities still retained ward boards that were relics of the old decentralized district system.

"Take the schools out of politics!" In the early twentieth century, that was the call to battle of advocates of a new concept of democracy in public education. These policy elites decided that the older concepts of common school governance and curriculum were antediluvian. Democracy, they insisted, did not mean laypeople running the schools, as trustees did all over the country. Democracy at its best meant administration of public schools by specially trained experts (superintendents and their staffs). A school system resembled a public hospital: a lay board might provide general oversight, but professionals should be in charge.

The reformers wanted to consolidate small rural districts and assert more control of country schools by counties and states. Taking city schools out of politics meant radically reducing the size of city school boards and abolishing ward boards.

As they sought to centralize and standardize education, they rejected the old idea that democracy demanded a common curriculum for all students. The intelligence and future destiny of pupils clearly differed, and thus the curriculum should be differentiated to match their abilities and needs. Democratic schools provided opportunities to all students to find niches suited to their various talents. Equality meant difference, not sameness, of treatment.

The public school, then, became an "instrument of democracy" run by apolitical experts, with authority "in the hands of those who will really represent the interests of the children." Such leaders would be able to educate all children according to their abilities and destiny in life. The people owned the schools, but experts ran them, just as corporate CEOs managed their firms. Such was the new version of democracy in governance: a socially and economically efficient system that adapted schooling to different kinds of students, thereby guaranteeing equality of opportunity.

The redefinition of democracy and reorganization of schools became the conventional wisdom of educators for the following decades. Big districts and big schools, they said, were better than small ones. A centralized, specialized administrative structure was more efficient and accountable than a decentralized, simple one. Differentiation of the curriculum into several tracks and hundreds of electives generated greater equality of opportunity for students of varied ability and for the numerous ethnic and "racial" groups.

Beginning in the 1960s, in another effort to change the course of history, reformers set out once again to redefine democracy and to challenge the organizational changes introduced in the first half of the twentieth century. They argued that small schools are better, that big districts should be decentralized, that all students should be helped to meet the same high academic standards, that academic segregation of students into tracks limits their learning, and that schools can benefit from parents' involvement in educational reform.

Reformers today recognize that no amount of wishful thinking can transform politics of education into neutral administration, for schooling is and always has been intrinsically value-laden. The question is not *whether* politics but *whose* politics. In the last fifty years the history of school governance is in large part the story of efforts to breach the buffers erected around schools during the first half of the twentieth century to protect them from participatory democracy.

Groups that were excluded or unfairly treated—for example, African Americans, Latinos, the handicapped, women—have organized in social movements and have sought access and influence in public education. Besides employing traditional political strategies, these new voices have also expanded notions of democracy; they speak, for example, of *cultural* democracy, of equal respect and equal rights for all cultural groups, and of *economic* democracy to close the gap between rich and poor school districts.

The politics of education has never been more fluid and complicated than today. As in earlier periods of contentiousness, some critics—especially various advocates of vouchers and school choice—have put a new spin on the concept of democracy. The challenge this time is even more fundamental than the earlier attempt to rely on experts. These critics do not seek to replace politics with professional administration. Indeed, they consider public education already too bureaucratic, too constrained by government regulations inflicted by special-interest groups.

The solution, they say, is to replace politics with markets. Treating schooling as a consumer good and giving parents vouchers for the education of their children solves the problem of quality and decision making: parents choose the schools that will best suit their children. The collective choices engendered by democratic institutions produced bureaucracy and gridlock, they say; the invisible hand of the market will lead the individual to the best personal choice. The market in education will satisfy and liberate families through competition.

But wait. Is education primarily a consumer good or a common good? *School* provides a context for answering that question. If Thomas Jefferson, Horace Mann, and John Dewey were now to enter policy discussions on public education, they might well ask if Americans have lost their way. Democracy is about making wise collective choices, not individual consumer choices. Democracy in education and education in democracy are not quaint legacies from a distant and happier time. They have never been more essential to wise self-rule than they are today.

DAVID TYACK

Introduction

Part One

1770-1900

THE COMMON SCHOOL

Introduction

CARL F. KAESTLE

The public school as we know it was born in the mid-nineteenth century. Its founders called it the "common" school. Common schools were funded by local property taxes, charged no tuition, were open to all white children, were governed by local school committees, and were subject to a modest amount of state regulation. They arose through two decades of debate prior to the Civil War in the Northeast and the Midwest of what is now the United States and, later in the nineteenth century, in the South and the West. But to understand those debates we must go back to eighteenth-century colonial America. There we can see how people handled education without public schooling.

In eighteenth-century America, the institutions closest to our public schools were the short-term schools supported by towns in the northern British colonies. Town meetings often voted to provide elementary schooling for ten or twelve weeks a year. They often favored boys over girls and charged parental fees to supplement the town's support. While this may seem like some partial precursor of the public schools, it is important to note that if we think of education more broadly conceived and not just as schooling, the colonial mode of education was very different from that of the late nineteenth century. Across all the colonies—French and Spanish colonies as well as in British America—schooling was less important in the education process than it was in the later, industrial world. These societies were largely agricultural. Work was learned on farms and plantations. Families carried most of the responsibility for children's learning, along with churches, neighbors, and peers. Not only was schooling less important and thus not very extensive, but in general it was not free, not governmental, and not secular. Some free education was available in the church charity schools of East Coast cities, the mission and presidio schools of the Southwest, and the town schools of the northern British colonies, but in many areas these schools were scarce and transitory. To the extent that education involved schooling, parents were responsible for it. They hired tutors, sent their toddlers to "dame schools" for the ABCs, joined other parents to support subscription schools, sent their children to a mission or charity school, or voted in town meetings to support schools on a year-to-year basis through a combination of parental fees and town support. Or they did nothing about schooling.

These arrangements meant that family wealth, race, and gender had a strong impact on how much formal education a child received. But did this colonial mode of education work well in these eighteenth-century societies? It did, in the sense that education was not a controversial public issue, and the education levels required of the work world were modest. The people who had a say in such matters—mostly male property owners—thought that leaving education in the hands of parents and churches was appropriate. Still, dynamic forces in the eighteenth century encouraged more schooling and more literacy. In the British colonies, Protestantism encouraged popular literacy, as did the cash economy that gradually spread outward from commercial cities. Political and economic tensions with England increased, and the colonists avidly read English and continental theorists on the nature of republics and balanced government. These passions spawned newspapers and political pamphlets. The franchise gradually expanded among white males, and by the time of the American Revolution, rudimentary literacy levels (measured crudely by the ability to sign one's name) were about 90 percent among white men and at least 60 percent among white women.

The idea that schooling depended on local and largely familial initiatives was a tradition firmly embedded in the colonies at the time of the American Revolution, but this colonial mode of education had proven capable of expansion. Nonetheless, some of the famous political leaders of that era—notably Thomas Jefferson, Benjamin Rush, and Noah Webster—were concerned about the uneven nature of schooling in different communities and anxious about the educational needs of the new nation. They thought that schooling should be not only more widespread but also more systematic and more publically supervised. They argued that the survival of the young republic depended upon educated citizens who could understand public issues, who would elect virtuous leaders, and who would sustain the delicate balance between liberty and order in the new political system.

Beneath the spirited discussions about these ideas, the colonial mode of education persisted, unperturbed. When Jefferson's plans for a state system of education in Virginia were rejected by the legislature, he complained about the "snail paced gait" of education reform. Rush's plans met a similar fate in the Pennsylvania legislature. New York State used profits from some public land sales to support local schooling in the 1790s, but when the money ran out, the program ended. Connecticut similarly distributed some funds from the sale of its Western Reserve lands, and Massachusetts had a weakly enforced 1789 law directing towns to provide elementary schools. The conditions in the new republic did not dispose people to change the way they educated their children, despite the rhetoric of their leaders about the fragility of the new government. The colonial mode of education was working well enough for most voters, and they did not want more government involvement in this matter.

By the 1840s, things had changed dramatically. The states of the Northeast were undergoing an industrial revolution. The number of cities in the region with a population of more than 10,000 increased from three in 1800 to forty-two by 1850. Textile production shot up. Canals and then railroads crisscrossed the area and the nation. Immigration swelled, bringing large numbers of Roman Catholics to a predominantly Protestant nation. These factors formed the necessary preconditions for the creation of public schools. The pace of change and the urgency of new social problems fostered the development of new institutions.

The Common School

The force of the changes was most visible and severe in the coastal and industrial cities, where alarmed reformers of the early national period adopted various approaches to problems of poverty and vice, some copied from England. The dominant mode was represented by nondenominational charity schools and tract societies, which treated poverty as a defect of character, not a defect of the system. Charity schools targeted the poor as a separate group, and they were governed by independent boards, not the government. In these respects they did not resemble public schools. On the other hand, in large cities like New York and Philadelphia, these charity schools were organized into centrally supervised systems, and they literally became the public schools in the mid-nineteenth century. At that point they attempted to move beyond their poor constituents to attract the children of more affluent parents. School reformers of that day denigrated the charity schools for isolating the poor, but they admired the highly organized urban systems that had evolved from them. This admiration of large, bureaucratized urban school systems was a staple among educational reformers for over a century.

Perhaps it is not fruitful to argue about whether the "true" prototype of the common school is the urban charity school of the early nineteenth century or the small-town school of colonial New England, but it is worth noting that in the Northeast there was a direct institutional connection between schools for the moral education of the urban poor and the public schools of the mid-nineteenth century. Some of this same impulse to address and regulate social deviance can be seen in the Whig Party's espousal of state institutions beyond the urban context, a repertoire that included not only canals, railroads, normal schools, and common schools but also prisons, almshouses, and insane asylums.

Although the Midwestern states were newer, more agricultural, and less densely populated, they joined in the common school movement. Many settlers had migrated from the Northeast, so they brought with them traditions of ad hoc town schools, but they also debated and ultimately adopted the more ambitious and governmental approach of the common school reforms. In doing so, they cited both eastern models and changes in other Midwestern states. Their region partook of the dynamic economic developments of the day: a transportation revolution that fostered national markets, the growth of cities, and the presence of large numbers of immigrants. These developments raised issues

School: 1770–1900

about moral education, common public values, and education for economic expansion. Towns competed with each other to develop their institutions, hoping to become county seats and rail centers. A heady mixture of capitalism, republican government, and religious diversity brought much conflict to antebellum America, but it also produced institutional innovation.

These conditions were necessary but not sufficient to establish the rudimentary state common school systems. That development took leadership and two decades of political struggle. Many voting Americans opposed the intervention of state government into the process of education, even in the 1840s and 1850s. People in small rural districts feared the interference of the state, as did some religious groups. The Congregationalists in Massachusetts and the Quakers in Indiana continued to shape the curriculum of local schools with their distinctive beliefs. The fears of these various opponents were well founded. Common school reformers moved gradually to force the consolidation of small districts into larger town systems and to eliminate sectarian religious practices from the schools, urging instead a more generalized Protestant version of Christianity. Party politics played a role as well. Horace Mann, Henry Barnard, and many other school reformers were Whigs, and many Democrats looked upon the common school reform as a Whig invention. They criticized its centralizing features as "Prussian" and argued for local control. Urban Catholics complained about the Protestant biases of the fledgling public schools, providing yet another source of opposition and a reproach to the reformers' claims that public schools were "common" to all.

Thus the debate was long and hard fought, in each state. In 1840 a predominantly Democratic opposition mustered 43 percent of the votes in the Massachusetts legislature in an effort to oust Horace Mann and abolish his position. Two years later a similar challenge in Connecticut succeeded, costing Henry Barnard his job. In some states, legislation to encourage consolidation of district schools was passed, then repealed, then passed again, over a period of years. Nonetheless, by 1860, across the Northeast and the Midwest, state laws established the position of state superintendent of instruction, with responsibilities to publicize educational causes and exemplary practices, collect and summarize statistics on education, and administer the new education laws of the state. The linchpin of the movement was laws requiring property tax support for free schools. Many states also encouraged or required district consolidation; some provided a modicum of state aid to the towns and support for teacher institutes. Some supervised teacher licensing; others provided county supervisors to oversee school practices.

Some earlier historians celebrated this achievement as a great victory for democracy, and they chastised its opponents as ignorant or mean-spirited. More recently, other historians have emphasized the negative side—the use of schools for cultural conformism, the continued inequalities, and the racism in the system—and they have characterized its opponents as victims. I look on the mid-nineteenth-century invention of public school systems as a highly contested development, politically fragile at the time, ultimately durable, and imperfect. It widened access, nudged schools toward longer sessions, and encouraged professional development. More important, it established the practice of using local property taxes to support public schools, eliminating tuition payments for parents but bequeathing to us a system that results in drastic variations in school expenditures across communities. The mid-nineteenth-century "common" school displayed not only financial inequalities but also cultural biases, racism, and gender discrimination, values challenged but still dominant in that day and beyond.

The common school movement moved education more fully into the public sphere and made it amenable to public policy. State system builders and urban centralizers seized the opportunity. While they attempted to coexist with local control, they also used legislation and supervision to encourage values they prized even more: free access to elementary and secondary education, a modest equalization of resources across localities, the assimilation of a diverse population, moral education for a stable society, more extensive education for a more complex economy, and the training of citizens in patriotism, political knowledge, and public affairs. Still, the policy choice was for a continuing compromise between central authority and local control—a uniquely American compromise. It was not divinely ordained, and it was not perfect. All systems have price tags. A majority of Americans opted in the nineteenth century for state-regulated school systems that retained a large measure of local control and funding. Other nations have more highly standardized national systems of education. Critics of the public schools in America today have urged the government to go in the opposite direction and subsidize more variety and choice among schools.

In my opinion, we don't profit much by arguing about whether the invention of public school systems was a Good Thing or a Bad Thing. We have the benefit of hindsight, but we can make judgments only through the lenses of our own values and experiences. Hindsight helps us look at the common school movement's best impulses and its greatest failings and see them not as immutable but as experimental. We can then examine today's public schools and attempt to fashion ways to make them more equal, inclusive, and effective for the kind of education we need in the twenty-first century. In our society, the way we provide common public schooling is inherently a compromise—a balance between competing, legitimate values. We must therefore strive continually to find a creative balance between local and central direction, between diversity and standards, between liberty and equality.

The Educated Citizen

If a nation expects to be ignorant and free,
it expects what never was and never will be.

THOMAS JEFFERSON

Boy walking to school, ca. 1820.
Artist unknown, oil on canvas.

In the thirteen colonies of pre-revolutionary America, only the larger towns in New England were required by law to build schools. Elsewhere, education was neither free nor public. Chester Finn, education policy expert, suggests that "if there were schools at all—and many communities had them and some didn't—there were schools because people in a particular town or village or section of a county decided they wanted to get together and pool their resources and hire a teacher. And thus you have the famous old stories about the teacher who was paid with two bushels of wheat and a half a cow."

Some colonial parents paid a fee to send their youngest children to "dame schools." Historian Nancy Hoffman tells us, "If you have ever seen those wonderful pictures of a sort of Mother Goose–

women for teachers

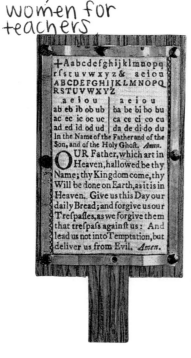

School: 1770–1900

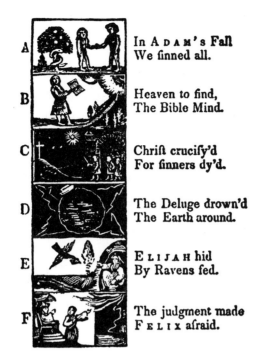

A	In ADAM'S Fall We finned all.
B	Heaven to find, The Bible Mind.
C	Chrift crucify'd For finners dy'd.
D	The Deluge drown'd The Earth around.
E	ELIJAH hid By Ravens fed.
F	The judgment made FELIX afraid.

Religious alphabet from The New England Primer.

like person with three or four kids clustered around her skirt, that is sort of the romanticized view of the dame school. It's probably something between learning your letters and learning some discipline and what we now call day care." Little children were given a "hornbook," which was a printed copy of the alphabet and a short prayer mounted on wood and covered with transparent cow horn. Most schooling was closely linked to the Protestant Bible, brought by early settlers to the New World.

The most common schoolbook was the *The New England Primer,* used by instructors to teach reading and the Protestant catechism. Some older boys went to grammar schools, where they studied mathematics, Latin, and philosophy. Only the most privi-

The Educated Citizen

leged had the means to continue on through college or university. By the time of the Revolutionary War, the vast majority of Americans were educated just enough to read the newspaper and the Bible, and figure their taxes.

Having won their independence from Britain, Americans rallied under the leadership of General George Washington. Ahead lay the difficult task of building a nation out of thirteen former colonies. Many believed that schools could play a critical role.

For Noah Webster, a teacher in Connecticut, the first step was to eliminate British textbooks from American classrooms. He wrote, "For America in her infancy to adopt the maxims of the old world would be to stamp the wrinkles of old age on the bloom of youth.... Begin with the infant in his cradle. Let the first word he lisps be Washington." In 1783, Webster published a textbook known as the "Blueback Speller." Webster's "Speller" promoted a new national language to be spelled and pronounced differently from British English. It sold millions of copies over the years and was a forerunner to Webster's *American Dictionary of the English Language.*

To leaders like Thomas Jefferson, the survival of the democracy depended on educating all Americans. As he put it, "Preach a crusade against ignorance.... Establish and improve the law for educating the common people.... General education will enable every man to judge for himself what will secure or endanger his freedom." Historian Diane Ravitch describes the ideals that underlay his commitment to general education: "Jefferson said that in a democracy the people vote and choose their rulers, and that means you have to learn to read and write and you have to learn enough of the foundations of education to be a citizen."

Jefferson had received the type of education available only to the wealthy of his time. Privately tutored as a child, he later graduated from the College of William and Mary in Virginia. In 1778, as a member of the Virginia Assembly, he drafted a proposal to guarantee three years of public schooling for all children, with advanced education for a select few. Author and journalist Nicholas Lemann explains the two-tiered system: "Jefferson's idea was a little bit of universal education with two purposes: One, to give people the democratic basics, and two, to be a kind of staging area or an audition site for this small group of natural aristocrats who would then be given a full-dress university education and then serve the country as he had done." Historian David Tyack adds, "As Jefferson put it, 'raking a few geniuses from the rubbish,' and giving them scholarships to go on to secondary school and then to the university would result in a meri-

Thomas Jefferson, proponent of universal education. Portrait by Charles Wilson Peale.

Double portrait of Mary Cary and Susan Elizabeth Johnson, 1848, oil on board mounted on panel, by William Mathew Prior (1806–1873).

tocracy in which the most able people could be educated—at public expense—up to a high level."

Jefferson didn't consider the possibility of female geniuses; his plan allowed three years of schooling for girls, enough to prepare them for marriage and motherhood. And he offered no education to slaves. For slaves, education was often a hidden and dangerous undertaking. Historian Vanessa Siddle Walker gives an example: "There was a sewing school . . . where the children came to school ostensibly to learn sewing and they would sit and they would sew, but of course underneath that material would be textbooks. And so even during slavery at risk of life, people were interested in trying to attain this magical something that we call literacy."

School: 1770–1900

Notwithstanding his views on blacks and women, Jefferson's ideas about education were considered radical. Virginia assemblymen scoffed at the notion of sending farmers to college. A wealthy Virginia planter suggested that "it is a great mistake to suppose there is more knowledge or utility in philosophy than in the agricultural or mechanical arts. Take away the food of man and his existence would cease. Take away his philosophy and he would scarcely know it was gone."

Jefferson persisted in trying to persuade the Virginia Assembly to ratify his education proposal. Three times between 1779 and 1817, Jefferson's "Bill for the More General Diffusion of Knowledge" came up for a vote. Each time, to his frustration, it was defeated. As he put it, "There is a snail-paced gait for the advance of new ideas. . . . People have more feeling for canals and roads than for education." Jefferson continued to push for public schooling, even as he served as secretary of state, vice president, and, finally, president. His final educational battle led to the creation of the state-supported University of Virginia. But his most powerful legacy was the argument that public education was essential to democracy. As he put it, "If a nation expects to be ignorant and free, it expects what never was and never will be."

In the 1830s and 1840s, Jefferson's dream of statewide school systems began to take root, most notably in Massachusetts through the work of a reformer named Horace Mann. Mann was the secretary of education for the state of Massachusetts, the first such official in the United States. As the majority leader of the

*Daguerreotype of Horace Mann. "The equalizing capacity of the school was
something that he very much believed in. The common school became for him the place
where we all come together, elite and poor." —Kathryn Kish Sklar, historian*

Massachusetts State Senate, Mann had been a builder of railroads and canals, and was in on the building of the insane asylum in Massachusetts. Historian Kathryn Kish Sklar describes his hands-on approach to overseeing the state's schools: "It is very interesting how Horace Mann has become our paragon for the promotion of public schools. He endeared himself to people in the nineteenth century by riding horseback from district to district and reviewing the actual physical facility."

Inspecting as many schools as he could, Mann found a system built on inequity. With no state supervision, schools varied widely from town to town. They were supported by local taxes and by fees charged to parents. Wealthy children could stay in school longer; the poorest couldn't afford to go at all. According to Mann, the

"Caught Napping."
Line drawing, 1866.

The Educated Citizen

Daguerreotype of boy and girl with books.

overall state of learning left much to be desired. Mann visited one thousand schools over the course of six years and wrote detailed reports on their physical condition. Most lacked adequate light, heat, and ventilation. Some were in such bad shape that Mann was surprised to find them standing at all. Of one school he wrote, "The schoolhouse in District No. 3. How shall we speak of that? Clear away the surrounding forest which protects it and before the next gale is over, the foundation stones would be all that remain of it. Already aware of the danger, the mice have forsaken it."

Other problems existed aside from the condition of the facilities. Schoolchildren spent hours sitting on hard benches, which Mann feared would damage their spines. There were no blackboards and no standardized textbooks, so pupils spent hours memorizing or reciting passages from books they brought from home, no matter how outdated or irrelevant. One book on penmanship devoted an entire page to the proper writing of the letter O, at a 53-degree slant. A geography text described a sea serpent found off the New England coast. The state took better care of its livestock, Mann concluded, than of its children in school: "You crowd from 40 to 60 children into that ill-constructed shell of a building, there to sit in the most uncomfortable seats that could

School: 1770–1900

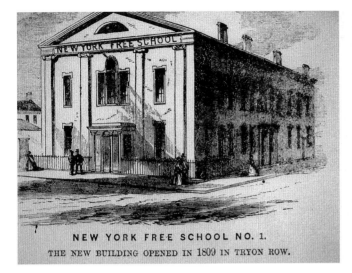

NEW YORK FREE SCHOOL NO. 1.
THE NEW BUILDING OPENED IN 1809 IN TRYON ROW.

Immigrant Education School Building, the first "public" school, built by the Free School Society in New York City in 1809. The upper room seated five hundred children.

be contrived, expecting that with the occasional application of the birch they will then come out educated for manhood or womanhood . . . ?"

From Cape Cod to the Berkshires, Mann held a series of public meetings to propose a new system of what he called "common schools." They would serve all boys and girls, and teach a common body of knowledge that would give each student an equal chance in life. "It is a free school system, it knows no distinction of rich and poor . . . it throws open its doors and spreads the table of its bounty for all the children of the state. . . . Education then, beyond all other devices of human origin, is the equalizer of the conditions of men, the great balance wheel of the social machinery."

Common schools would be free of charge, so that poor children could attend. They would be of the highest quality, to draw wealthier students away from private schools. Standards would be set

Studio portrait of Teacher Orva Haskin Smith and her students.

and enforced by the state, and the system would be entirely funded with tax dollars. Mann's plan was instantly and vigorously opposed because it imposed state control over traditionally local concerns, and imposed a tax burden on all citizens. Nicholas Lemann describes the basis for this resistance: "If you go back and read the history and Horace Mann's writing and so on, it impresses on you the precariousness of this basic idea that we take for granted, that all citizens have an obligation to reach into their wallet and pay for children to be educated even if they're not their own children."

Mann gained a wider audience through the annual reports he wrote while serving on the board of education. He recommended many of the things we associate with schools today: chairs with backs, a bell, a blackboard, standardized textbooks. Mann's writings were read and debated from New England to the Southwest, from Europe to South America. His ideas on school reform made him one of the most influential writers of his time, and his victories included state bureaus of education, teacher training, and free tax-supported education for many children in the northern states. Author and educator E. D. Hirsch summarizes Mann's achievements: "Horace Mann is rightly the patron saint of public education, not because of what he always managed to accomplish in Massachusetts but because of what he said in those reports. He talked about the public schools having this leveling effect, that merit should be able to rise. There is, I think, a deep connection between Mann's vision and Jefferson's because both of them disliked the idea of the family you were being born into determining how you ended up in American life."

Even as the common school movement got under way, conflict arose over the question of religion. Growing numbers of immigrants were arriving from Europe. By 1840, nearly half of New York City residents were foreign born. Many were Irish Catholics, who were generally poor and desperate for an education. Yet in New York, they found that the public schools, while free and open to all, were effectively, Protestant. "All the Protestant sects could feel very comfortable in American public schools," says historian

The Educated Citizen

"Assembled for Morning Exercises." Grammar School No. 56, New York City.

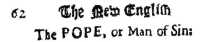

62 **The New English**
The POPE, or Man of Sin:

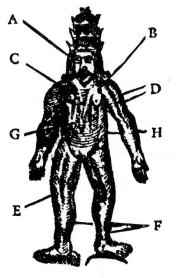

A
B
C
D
G
H
E
F

Diane Ravitch. "If you read Horace Mann you will see that his idea was we should have no sectarianism in the schools—we should all read the same Bible. We should all say the same prayers, we should use those religious ideas that are common to all of us—meaning all of us Protestants." As Father Richard Shaw, a church historian, says, "Irish Catholic children were being expected to attend schools where the King James Bible was read, where Protestant hymns were being sung, where prayers were being recited, but most importantly where textbooks and the entire slant of the teaching was very much anti-Irish and very much anti-Catholic."

At Old St. Patrick's Cathedral in New York, Bishop John Hughes launched a protest. A forty-three-year-old Irish immigrant known as "Dagger John," Hughes was fierce and uncompromising. He proclaimed, "We are unwilling to pay taxes for the purpose of destroying our religion in the minds of our children. That such books should be put into [their] hands [is] unjust, unnatural, and intolerable." Father Shaw describes the effect of the schools' anti-Catholic bias: "That created a situation in which

"The Pope, or Man of Sin," from The New England Primer, ca. 1737. "There are statements in public school textbooks that would just astound you today. 'Catholics return from Communion invigorated for the perpetuation of new offenses.' 'The Irish immigration has emptied out the common sewers of Ireland into our waters' and so forth."
—Carl Kaestle, historian

issue of taxes when people don't support what's being taught in schools

The Educated Citizen

33

Bishop John Hughes.
"Bishop Hughes felt that
the Catholic children
in those schools would be
subjected to an indoctrination
into the Protestant faith
and he was right."
—Diane Ravitch, historian

some twenty thousand children were running the streets of New York without benefit of education because they refused to be part of a system biased against themselves."

These children deserved their own schools, Bishop Hughes believed. He demanded that the New York Public School Society, the Protestant civic leaders in charge of education, make city funds available for Catholic schools. When Jews and Presbyterians also asked for funds, city leaders agreed to hold a debate. "The great school debates in New York City in 1840 were amazing if for

School: 1770–1900

Children in yard of Home for the Friendless, a New York orphanage, ca. 1860s.

no other reason than they packed the galleries. This was great entertainment for all of New York City," Shaw tells us. "More significant was that it was one man against a whole army of people. Different ministers of different denominations kept spelling one another and coming after Hughes, and hour after hour, evening after evening, he would stand up and rebut them." Bishop Hughes exclaimed to the crowds, "We will not send our children where they will be trained up without religion, lose respect for their parents and the faith of their fathers, and come out turning up their noses at the name of Catholic.... In a word, give us our just proportion of the common school fund!"

The debate continued in the press, where many readers spoke out against public funding for religious schools. In November 1841, an editorial writer for the *New York Herald* wrote, "Once we admit that the Catholics have a right to a portion of the school fund, every other sect will have the same right.... We shall be convulsed with endless jarrings and quarrels about the distribution of it, and little left for the public schools." A citizen's letter to the editor agreed: "The Catholics have a right to think and worship in their own way, but have no right to claim one cent of the public money to propagate their own faith." Controversy over the use of the Protestant Bible in the public schools escalated nationwide. In Pennsylvania in 1844, a Catholic church was burned to the ground and thirteen people were killed in a conflict known as the Philadelphia Bible Riots.

But change was under way. After the City Hall debates, school

OUR COMMON SCHOOLS AS THEY ARE AND AS THEY MAY BE.—[See Page 141.]

"Once we admit that the Catholics have a right . . . every other sect will have the same right. We shall be convulsed with endless jarrings and quarrels." —New York Herald *editorial, November 1841*

principals in New York were ordered to search through textbooks for passages offensive to Catholics, which they painstakingly removed by hand. Two years later, the Public School Society was replaced by the newly formed New York City Board of Education, an elected body. Growing numbers of Catholic children enrolled. Meanwhile, John Hughes was named archbishop of New York in 1850, and he used his considerable power to help create a privately funded national system of Catholic schools. It became the major alternative school system in the United States.

The issue of religion took its place alongside other crucial issues facing the architects of public education, most notably that of race. In the years just prior to the Civil War, two-thirds of African Americans lived in the South, most of them as slaves with little or no access to education. In the North, blacks were entitled to

School: 1770–1900

Dismissal at 3:00 P.M., Grammar School No. 3, New York City.

LEFT *Engraving of*
African American boy
writing by candlelight.

BELOW *Interior School*
Room No. 2, Colored
Orphan Asylum,
Good Friday, 1861.

attend public school. Yet they were often prohibited from attending school with whites and were instead segregated in separate and usually inferior facilities.

The African American community in Boston, Massachusetts, had a long history of fighting for the abolition of slavery and for equal access to the city's public schools. But in the 1840s, black primary schoolchildren were still restricted to just two schools in Boston, both segregated. Parents and reformers gathered at the African Meeting House to debate strategies for protest. They were encouraged by escaped slave and noted abolitionist Frederick Douglass, who wrote, "The point we must aim at is to obtain admission for our children in to the nearest school house, and the best school house in their own neighborhood." Historian James Anderson explains the importance of education to African Americans at this time, despite the fact that they would be denied equal opportunities: "It became clear to most of them that a better education would not mean a better position in society, or a better job. They knew that they couldn't get into the trades in most places, so they began to redefine the very purpose of education. African Americans began to tie the quest for freedom and the quest for education and

From the Anti-Slavery Alphabet, a children's book, 1847.

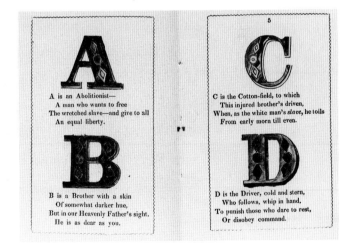

A is an Abolitionist—
A man who wants to free
The wretched slave—and give to all
An equal liberty.

B is a Brother with a skin
Of somewhat darker hue,
But in our Heavenly Father's sight,
He is as dear as you.

C is the Cotton-field, to which
This injured brother's driven,
When, as the white man's *slave*, he toils
From early morn till even.

D is the Driver, cold and stern,
Who follows, whip in hand,
To punish those who dare to rest,
Or disobey command.

The Educated Citizen

excellence together. And so they began to think of education as part of the freedom struggle."

In the winter of 1846, a group of nearly ninety African Americans drew up a petition to the Boston School Committee that called for an immediate end to segregation in the city's public schools. It read in part, "The establishment of separate schools for our children deprives us of those equal privileges and advantages to which we are entitled as citizens. These separate schools cost more and do less for the children. We therefore earnestly request that our children be allowed to attend schools in the Districts in which we live." In response, the school committee investigated the state of the black schools. In their report they revealed many deficiencies: "The school rooms are too small, the paint much defaced, the apparatus is so shattered it cannot be used." Despite the report, no action was taken.

Soon after the school committee's investigation, five-year-old Sarah Roberts was assigned to the Smith School. Her father, Benjamin Roberts, tried to enroll Sarah in a better school closer to home. Her application was denied. Roberts then tried the other four schools that Sarah would pass on her walk to the Smith School. At each, she was refused admission. Once, she was physically ejected by a teacher. Members of the school committee defended segregation, claiming that it was maintained for "the special benefit of colored children." In the words of the committee, "In the case of colored children, we maintain that their peculiar physical, mental and moral structure requires an educational

School: 1770–1900

Sally and George Davis Washington. "There wasn't anybody too old or too young who didn't feel as though he or she couldn't benefit from some level of education." —Vanessa Siddle Walker, historian

treatment different from that of white children." Outraged, Roberts vowed to sue the City of Boston, naming his daughter Sarah as plaintiff.

Some African Americans opposed Roberts's efforts. "Integration would bring colored children into competition with more advanced and wealthy white children," wrote one opponent, adding that it might result in "sneers, insults, assaults and jeers." Another black Bostonian added, "What kind of education would our children receive from a white teacher? The Smith School should simply hire a black teacher with a college degree." James Anderson explains: "There were many people in the African American communities who simply said we don't have a ghost of a chance to achieve integrated education. And so let's develop a full-fledged quality system of education even though it is segregated. And then there were others who said, we cannot accept this position in society because we will be doomed forever."

With the majority of African Americans in favor of integration, Roberts filed his suit. By 1849 the case reached the Massachusetts State Supreme Court. Representing Roberts were Robert Morris, one of the nation's first African American lawyers, and abolitionist lawyer Charles Sumner. "The school is the little world in which the child is trained for the larger world of life, beginning there those relations of Equality which the constitution and the laws promise to all," Sumner argued. "I conclude that there is but one kind of public school, free to all, whether rich or poor, whether Catholic or Protestant, whether white or black—excluding none,

comprehending all." Chief Justice Lemuel Shaw ruled against Sarah Roberts. Undeterred, Roberts and a group called the Negro School Abolition Society took their cause to the state legislature. In 1855, a law was passed abolishing segregation in the schools of Massachusetts. It was the first such law in the nation.

The Roberts case was a foundation on which others would build. In 1896, the U.S. Supreme Court cited Judge Shaw's decision when it permitted segregation on the grounds that separate could be equal. In 1954, the Supreme Court cited Charles Sumner in _Brown v. Board of Education_, the case that finally launched the desegregation of American public schools. Of those who brought the Roberts case, James Anderson explains, "They were the

"Reconstruction was as Booker T. Washington described it: an entire race trying to go to school."
—*Vanessa Siddle Walker, historian*

dreamers. They were the ones who believed in an America that was hard to imagine, an America without race discrimination. An America in which all people irrespective of race, creed, or color would have equal access to public institutions, public places. They were dreamers."

Issues of race and schooling would only become more urgent in the last quarter of the nineteenth century. The Civil War ended in 1865. Four million Americans, formerly slaves, were now free. As we learn from Vanessa Siddle Walker, "Reconstruction was, as Booker T. Washington described it, an entire race trying to go to school. There wasn't anybody too old or too young that didn't feel as though he or she couldn't benefit from some level of schooling and it was seen as the most valuable undertaking—the notion of going to school."

American flag with country school image.

During this same period, a vast movement of settlers into the western United States was intensifying the demand for schools.

"What you had was a group of people as they moved west, as they went in their Conestoga wagons, or went around the Horn, who wanted to reproduce the institutions that they remembered in the East," explains David Tyack. "As you look across the new states as they were created in the Middle West and the Plains States and the far Pacific Coast, the states talked forever about education as an absolutely essential means of creating a stable, and prosperous and virtuous republic. So

that after the Civil War, the Congress actually required states to guarantee in their constitutions that they would offer a free non-sectarian education to all children." "Schools became important civic amenities that could draw settlers," notes historian Kathryn Kish Sklar. "As people migrated ... they founded their own towns, they invested their money in those locations and then they hoped that their town would be a success. It was important to them to have something to offer settlers and attract them, and a school was a very important institution that they could offer."

On the frontier, families were widely scattered. Some school districts covered a thousand miles. Getting to school could take

Sod school, Logan County, Colorado, 1909. Frontier schools were set up in saloons, sod dugouts—wherever space was available.

frontier Schools

grit, determination, and, at times, ingenuity. In wealthier settlements, schools were built as ornaments to success. More often, classes convened in sod dugouts, defunct saloons, and wherever else space could be found. In this vast territory, with new schools cropping up everywhere, a crisis arose: who would teach the children of the settlers?

Advocate Catharine Beecher promoted female teachers as a civilizing force in the West. A member of a prominent New England

*Daguerreotype of Catharine Beecher, 1848. "She argued for female teachers, to create a profession for the women of her time that would be as great as medicine or law for men."
—Carl Kaestle, historian*

The Educated Citizen

Daguerreotype of classroom in the Emerson School for Girls.

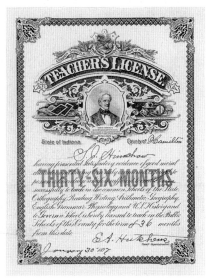

ABOVE *Miss Blanche Lamont with her school at Hecla, Montana, 1893.*

LEFT *Teacher's license, Hamilton County, Indiana, 1897.*

Schoolchildren playing a circle game with their teacher, Miss Sherman.
Pine Creek School, Livingston, Montana, area, 1898.

family and sister of author Harriet Beecher Stowe, Catharine Beecher saw teaching as a woman's moral calling: "God designed women to be the chief educators of our race.... It is woman who is fitted by disposition and habits and circumstances for such duties." Beecher founded colleges to educate women in philosophy, science, and mathematics and train them for service out west. Kathryn Kish Sklar brings to light Beecher's influence: "She really made teaching respectable for middle-class women. She was an elite person who advocated that this was really a very appropriate behavior for a young woman to leave her family and go and live in another community and board around as a teacher. This was not on the face of it necessarily what a respectable young woman who wanted to make a good marriage would think to do."

Determined and educated, an army of young women teachers headed west. Nothing could have prepared them for the conditions they found upon arrival in their lonely outposts. One young lady witnessed a gunfight outside her classroom. Another found herself boarding in a two-room cabin with a family of ten. Ellen P. Lee of Hamilton County, Indiana, wrote about her teaching experience, "Nearly all the people are kind to me, but have not had an

Report card, 1890. Children had to master a great deal more than the three Rs.

An arithmetic class taught by Carrie Southworth at Morton School near Groton, New York, 1907.

opportunity for improving their minds. So they are very ignorant ... many of the adults can neither read nor write. Some cannot tell one letter from another. And so it is with the children." Ethel Hall Besquette of Tulare County, California, wrote of her classroom, "There are many openings in the walls of our school that admit birds, lizards, mice and snakes. During one lesson a snake appeared in the opening above a window, sticking his tongue out at us. I disposed of him amidst great applause." Kathryn Kish Sklar describes how women changed what went on in the classroom: "[The hiring of women] created a new ethic in schools that

School: 1770–1900

was feminized in which the teacher cared for the students—the teacher was not only a disciplinarian but also offered, not exactly the comforts of home, but a lot of the similar ingredients that had gone on in home schooling a century before that."

In their classrooms, such as they were, women teachers gave children on the remote frontier an introduction to literature, standards of behavior, and national ideals. In these tasks they relied on a series of textbooks written expressly for the children of the West, known as McGuffey readers. These readers, which eventually sold over 122 million copies, consisted of "moral tales," says

ABOVE *Little boy reciting in front of class, Morton School, near Groton, New York.*

RIGHT *"Peck's Bad Boy in School." Niagara Falls, New York, 1890.*

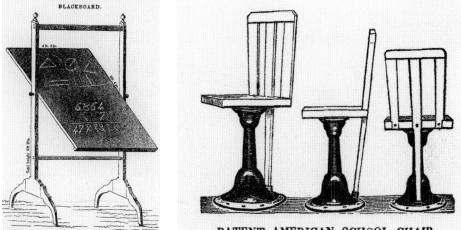

BLACKBOARD.

PATENT AMERICAN SCHOOL CHAIR.

historian Joel Spring. "The idea was that while the students learned how to read, they also learned the morality that would be this common morality of society.... And that is the idea that if you should work hard and acquire wealth then you are blessed by God." Such a lesson is apparent in a passage from McGuffey's *Third Eclectic Reader,* revised edition, 1879: "Lesson 40: Charlie and Rob. 'Don't you hate splitting wood?' asked Charlie. 'No, I rather like it,' said Rob. 'It's a tough job and it's nice to conquer it.' Now which of these boys do you think grew up to be a rich and

LEFT *School blackboard. From* The School and the Schoolmaster, *1858.*

RIGHT *Drawing of school chair. From* Common School Journal, *ca. 1840.*

The Educated Citizen

useful man and which of them joined a party of tramps before he was thirty years old?"

Capping off the school year was the annual spring exhibition when parents and friends gathered to review the work of America's teachers and the lessons being taught. By this time, students had to master a great deal more than the three Rs. The curriculum included physiology, an old-fashioned term for health and hygiene, biology, zoology, and even ichthyology for the upper grades. A favorite event was the spelling bee. Standing before a rapt audience, students competed fiercely over the spelling of exotic words such as "argillaceous" (of the nature of clay), "tetrastoon" (a four-sided court with porticoes), and "acephalous" (without a head).

The end of the nineteenth century saw explosive growth in America's public schools. Public school expenditures rose from $69 million in 1870 to $147 million in 1890. Public school enrollment increased from 7.6 million in 1870 to 12.7 million in the same decades. The United States was providing more schooling to more children than any other nation on earth, thanks in large part to the nineteenth-century movement for school reform. Yet not all children could attend public schools together. Many Native Americans were sent to special government schools, where they were forced to abandon tribal languages, customs, and dress. African Americans also faced exclusion, and many created their own schools. Despite hardship, black literacy soared in the decades after the Civil War, from 5 percent to 70 percent.

The great American experiment of universal education was well

under way. Inspired by Thomas Jefferson, promoted and refined by Horace Mann, Catharine Beecher, and others, America's public schools were a tremendous achievement with great promise for all. It remained to be seen how that promise would be met, as schools faced the enormous challenges of the twentieth century.

School: 1770–1900

Part Two

1900-1950

AS

AMERICAN

AS

PUBLIC

SCHOOL

Introduction

DIANE RAVITCH

In the 1960s and 1970s, it became fashionable to mock the assimilative function of the public school, but I know from personal experience that one of the greatest glories of the public school was its success in Americanizing immigrants. My mother was an immigrant from Bessarabia who arrived in the United States in 1917 at the age of nine with her mother and sister; her father had earlier traveled to Houston, Texas, where he was working as a tailor. My father, who grew up in Savannah, Georgia, was a child of Polish immigrants. The American public school was their portal to opportunity. They and their parents were part of a great wave of immigration from Europe that transformed America. And the institution that transformed them was the American public school. Through the public school, they learned English and they learned to be Americans. That was no small feat.

The first half of the twentieth century was a time of remarkable expansion for the American public school. Schools were called upon to teach the skills and knowledge needed for participation in a democratic industrial society to a rapidly growing and diverse population. At the opening of the twentieth century, nearly all children attended elementary school. At the midpoint of the century, nearly 80 percent of teenagers were enrolled in high school. The United States led the world in fulfilling the promise of universal access to schooling.

Yet even as school enrollments multiplied, questions continually arose about what to teach, whether to give the same kind of education to all children, and how to allocate educational opportunities among different groups of children. The debates of this period centered on differing ideas about what sort of education a democratic society should offer its children.

In 1900, the public school was one of the most treasured public institutions in the United States. Americans celebrated their tax-supported free schools as a quintessential symbol of the nation's democratic promise that all girls and boys could improve themselves and rise in the world in accordance with their talents and effort.

At this time, most children left school by the end of eighth grade to go to work or help out at home. The American common school usually offered eight years of instruction. With its emphasis on the three Rs, its reliance on rote recitations and spelling bees, its close ties to the citizenry, its underpaid teachers, and its usually crowded classrooms, it was a vital community institution. No education profession as such existed; local school boards made all important decisions about personnel and curriculum; teachers had little training or supervision. State departments of education had few employees and no control over local school boards, and federal education officials did little more than collect and disseminate statistics about education.

As the economy became more complex, students stayed in school longer to gain additional skills and knowledge. More and more districts established secondary schools, and high school enrollments increased dramatically in the early decades of the twentieth century. Education experts debated whether these new students should be expected to take the standard academic curriculum. The urgency of their debate heightened as high school enrollments soared, doubling every decade from 1890 to 1930. The extension of educational opportunity to so many youngsters was a triumph for the principle of universal education. An ever larger proportion of the population had the opportunity to attend secondary schools (though many African American youngsters lived in communities in the South where no high schools were available for them until mid-century).

School: 1900–1950

A significant share of the new public school enrollment was due, especially in the nation's cities, to a large tide of immigration from southern and eastern Europe, beginning in the late 1880s and continuing until about 1920. In the first decade of the new century, the majority of students in most urban centers were either immigrants or the children of immigrants. Two-thirds of the children in the public schools in New York City and Chicago, for example, had foreign-born fathers. That most of these newcomers had immigrated from southern and eastern Europe instead of northern and western Europe was considered ominous by some native-born Americans. The "old" immigration had come from such nations as Britain, Germany, and Scandinavia; the "new" immigration included large numbers of Russians, Poles, Jews, and Italians. Many prominent figures complained in books, articles, and legislative hearings that the "new" immigration consisted of undesirable "racial stock" as compared to the old and that it tended to be illiterate, criminal, dependent, and ill-fitted to the demands of a Teutonic civilization. A hue and cry arose in the popular media to restrict immigration, which Congress eventually did in the 1920s.

While politicians argued over immigration policy, immigrant children enrolled in the public schools. They or their parents understood that education was the likeliest route to improving their future lives in America. The schools, in turn, had to address the problems of these children, many of whom spoke no English and lived in slums, where housing and sanitary conditions were terrible. Many big-city public schools implemented programs to teach children how to be Americans, which meant regular health inspections and lessons in English, American history, and hygienic practices. Some school districts, like New York City, offered adult education classes, special classes for children with disabilities, and after-school programs.

As immigration reached its height in the prewar era, the progressive social reform movement also reached its apex. Some progressive reformers fought to improve living conditions, schools, and working conditions in the cities. Other progressives, however, crusaded for greater efficiency in municipal affairs and the schools. This latter group of school reformers successfully centralized and bureaucratized school administration and put expert professionals in control of the schools while simultaneously limiting the involvement of laypeople and parents. These efficiency-minded reformers, in alliance with business groups, advocated industrial and vocational education in the public schools, targeted

As American As Public School

especially at "hand-minded" immigrant children. The partisans of social efficiency clamored to reduce the years of common school education from eight to six, so that children as young as twelve could begin training for jobs (this was the rationale for the creation of "junior" high schools). Demands for industrial and vocational education were so insistent in the early years of the twentieth century that Congress enacted a federal program to aid vocational education in 1917.

The dramatic growth of school enrollments in the early decades of the century led to a search for new ways to educate the new students, particularly the children from immigrant and working-class backgrounds whose English was poor or who seemed unsuited for traditional academic courses. Many children were left back when they were unable to keep up with other children of their age, and they were considered "overage" for their grade. Such problems demanded new thinking, which was promptly supplied by efficiency experts in the nation's new schools of pedagogy. These experts believed that their methods of analysis were scientific and superior to academic traditionalism. They concluded that the curriculum itself was the problem, that it was based too much on verbal studies and academic subjects, and that these children needed practical studies to prepare them for jobs. Convinced that the children were repelled by purely intellectual pursuits, the experts recommended differentiation of the curriculum into multiple vocational tracks, and many school districts introduced numerous specialized occupational programs for children who were expected to become industrial and commercial workers, domestic workers, and housewives.

The process of guiding children into specialized curricular tracks was facilitated after World War I by the widespread dissemination of group intelligence tests. The tests were first used during the war to identify future officers, then marketed to the public schools as a tool to facilitate the assignment of children to different ability groups and different curricula. With few exceptions, the nation's leading psychologists of education (such as Edward L. Thorndike of Teachers College, Columbia University; Robert Yerkes of Harvard University; and Lewis Terman of Stanford University) collaborated in designing intelligence tests and promoting them as instruments that could correctly identify students' innate, fixed intelligence. The results of the Army I.Q. tests, which demonstrated differences among racial and national groups, were used as propaganda in the public campaign to restrict immigration. In the public schools, the I.Q. tests offered a seemingly scientific basis for assigning students to varying curricular tracks, allegedly in keeping with their "needs."

Psychological experts believed that the tests were the acme of educational science and that they would make the schools more efficient and rational in their use of resources. Critics of the tests, such as educator William Chandler Bagley and journalist Walter Lippmann, warned against their misuse, suggesting that they reflected differences in educational opportunities and should not serve to restrict future opportunities. The intelligence tests, however, were soon deeply embedded in education practice and even served as the model for the Scholastic Aptitude Test (SAT), which was used as a screening device for college admissions beginning in 1941.

At the same time that the nation's public schools became embroiled in classifying students for different curricular tracks, many private schools were created to experiment with the child-centered methods championed by philosopher John Dewey at his University of Chicago laboratory school at the turn of the century. Dewey achieved fame for his exposition of "learning by doing," and many small progressive schools were established to demonstrate that a highly individualized approach built around children's interests and the social life of the children's community would prove to be more educative than traditional academic studies. Progressive child-centered methods sometimes seeped into public schools as well, as public schools experimented with activity programs in the elementary grades and interdisciplinary programs in secondary schools.

Unfortunately, the term "progressive" was invoked to cover a multitude of programs, approaches, and methods, including not only child-centered schooling but also I.Q. testing, curricular sorting, and vocational education. Throughout the first half of the century, any efforts to diversify the curriculum away from academic studies and to restrict such studies only to college-bound students was considered "progressive."

One ill-fated progressive reform was the Gary Plan, first implemented in Gary, Indiana, by William Wirt, a former student of John Dewey. Wirt's program divided the day into alternating periods of study and work. Dewey hailed this approach in his influential book *Schools of Tomorrow*. Known as the "platoon system" (because children rotated among different facilities in the

As American As Public School

67

school), the Gary Plan met a ruinous end in New York City. A progressive mayor directed the board of education to install the Gary Plan in a number of schools in poor neighborhoods. Thinking that their children would be denied the chance to prepare for higher education, immigrant parents rioted in the midst of the 1917 mayoral campaign; consequently, the reform mayor was defeated, the Gary Plan was ousted from New York City, and its luster was irreparably tarnished.

By the 1930s and 1940s, the nation's schools had reached a point of apparent equilibrium in their programs: access to schooling was nearly universal, and students were tested for their intellectual aptitude and then assigned to the appropriate vocational or academic track. This procedure of assigning children to different curricular tracks in eighth or ninth grade was considered scientific at the time, even though it shunted large numbers of students away from the study of history, literature, foreign languages, or advanced courses in math and science. Nonetheless, for many children from impoverished circumstances, the public schools offered bountiful opportunity for advancement despite vocational tracking. The "system" appeared to work well indeed. The economic depression of the 1930s made the security of a teaching job attractive, despite low pay, but World War II brought about a massive teacher shortage as well as neglect of school construction and maintenance.

In the early 1940s, encouraged by their success at accommodating the needs of the nation's large population, educators saw yet another horizon to conquer, and they sought to revise the curriculum to retain unmotivated students. This laudable desire gave birth to something called the "life adjustment movement," in which leading educators proposed to turn public schooling into a mechanism for social engineering, an agency that would test students and guide them to appropriate occupational destinations. The leaders of the life adjustment movement proposed that only 20 percent of students should be prepared for higher education, another 20 percent should be prepared for skilled work, and the remaining 60 percent should get "life adjustment education," a program concentrated on the basic skills of everyday living, such as family life and consumer choices. As the recommendations for life adjustment education picked up momentum, its advocates claimed that it would be the best education not only for unmotivated students but for all students.

The anti-intellectualism inherent in this diagnosis for America's schools and children soon prompted a loud, negative reaction. A torrent of books and articles appeared in the late 1940s and early 1950s, ridiculing the emptiness and pretentiousness of life adjustment education. The most important of these books was Arthur Bestor's *Educational Wastelands*, which called for the restoration of a traditional academic curriculum for all students. The critics complained that the life adjusters had watered down the curriculum for all students, not just the laggard few. In 1955, just as criticism of the schools seemed to have crested, Rudolph Flesch's *Why Johnny Can't Read* appeared; Flesch blasted "whole word" reading methods and called for a return to phonics. The book was on national best-seller lists for nearly six months and inspired a ground-level battle between proponents of phonics methods and whole-word/whole-language methods that has become a recurrent feature of American education.

The public schools had never experienced anything like the popular critiques of the 1950s. Until then, the administrative reformers of the early part of the century had successfully limited lay influence in the schools and persuaded the public that education was a matter best left to the experts. But in the 1950s, complaints about the quality of education in the public schools were unrelenting, and critics blamed the schools' failings on education professors and their abiding hostility to substantive academic courses. The critics said that the experts' desire to make the schools more like "real life" had lowered standards, diminished students' effort, and reduced achievement. Defenders of the progressive approaches associated with life adjustment education responded vigorously to the critics, claiming that the public schools were doing as well as ever and meeting the needs of a larger and more diverse student population.

Very likely the charges and countercharges would have eventually died down as the debate grew stale. But when the Soviet Union managed to launch *Sputnik*, the first space satellite, the schools were immediately portrayed in the popular press as the institution at fault for the United States' failure to beat its Cold War rival into outer space. The public response to the Soviets' technological coup was outrage, and the schools became the scapegoat for the nation's wounded pride. Congress responded to *Sputnik* by passing the National Education Defense Act in 1958, which provided federal funding for graduate students of mathematics, sciences, and foreign languages, as well as money for new school construction. There was a brief flurry of interest in higher academic standards in the schools, but this enthusiasm waned within a few years as the schools were overtaken by the political and social turbulence of the 1960s.

The period from 1900 to 1957 was marked by both triumph and failure for the American public school. Its greatest success was its ability to expand and absorb millions of children, making elementary and secondary schooling nearly universal and providing educational opportunities to children across the nation. Its greatest failures were of two sorts: One was the consequence of an educational philosophy that accepted too easily the hereditarian claims of intelligence testers and that legitimated the apportioning of schooling to different groups of students on the grounds of test results. The other was the consequence of a tradition of intense localism, which failed to challenge racial segregation throughout the South and border states, and which became an immovable barrier to the establishment of any meaningful academic standards. *De jure* racial segregation was eventually declared unconstitutional by the U.S. Supreme Court in 1954; the failure to grapple with either state or national curriculum standards remained as a legacy for the balance of the century.

Despite its many problems, the successes of the American public school system in the first half of the century impressed other industrial nations, who saw the economic value of universal education and exerted themselves to catch up. The American school system's readiness to meet the challenge of numbers and to provide social mobility to low-income students was truly remarkable; its efforts to assimilate newcomers into American society were largely successful. Illiteracy declined sharply during these years, and educational attainment rose steadily. These were the enduring accomplishments of the American public school.

Not only did the public school transform the immigrants; the immigrants eventually helped to transform America, making landmark contributions in every walk of life, as artists, scientists, intellectuals, journalists, business leaders, professionals, and ordinary citizens. Not everyone, of course, achieved eminence, but everyone had a chance to be part of American society. That opportunity was the work of the school, the fruits of education.

To me, the most radical of all American ideas is the idea that everyone can be educated—not just that everyone can go to school, but that everyone can be educated. The American public school offered that promise in the first half of the twentieth century, and it remains a goal yet unfulfilled.

School: 1900–1950

70

"You Are an American"

We want our Kinder to learn mit der book, der paper,

und der pencil, not mit der sewing und der shop!

IMMIGRANT MOTHER FROM BROOKLYN

New York schoolchildren registering, 1913.

By 1900 the United States was becoming increasingly urban. Cities were crowded with immigrants arriving from every part of the globe. Between 1890 and 1930, over 22 million came to the United States, including almost three million children. For them, school was the place where the American dream was nurtured, and the future itself took shape. Hylda Burton immigrated to Gary, Indiana: "I was born in England. I came over on the *Olympic,* which was the sister ship to the *Titanic.* The *Olympic* stayed afloat, and as you know the *Titanic* went down. My father was out of work and so he decided that, to give us a better chance at education, actually to bring us over to America."

Jewish war orphans arriving from eastern Europe, 1921.

Writer Alfred Kazin, whose parents immigrated to Brooklyn, New York, remembers, "I hated school, partly because I was not a very good student. I was terrible at math, for example, which was a terror to me. The neighborhood was composed mostly of Jewish immigrants, from Russia and Poland. And there was a tremendous pressure on all the time to get an education." Julian Nava's parents immigrated to Los Angeles: "My mother and father were born in Mexico. We spoke only Spanish at home. I remember many of my

*Industrial school
in West 52nd Street,
ca. 1898.*

teachers, even Mrs. Acke whom I still care for. She gave me a very strong scolding and a swat, a spank in class . . . because she caught me speaking Spanish. And she said, 'Julian, speak English—you are an American.'"

So powerful was the lure of education that on the day after a steamship arrived, as many as 125 children would apply to one New York school. Thousands of students attended school part time for lack of space. Some classrooms were as crowded as tenements. Yet for many other children, school was nothing more than a mysterious building passed on the way to work. In 1900, only 50 percent of America's children were in school, and they received an

"You Are an American"

A class in the condemned Essex Street Market School, ca. 1898.

Night school in the Seventh Avenue Lodging House, ca. 1898.

average of only five years of schooling. The remaining children could often be found at work. Despite efforts at reform, as late as 1910 an estimated two million children held jobs. Not all considered this a hard-ship. David Tyack tells a story about a fac-tory inspector "who found children who legally were supposed to be in school. But she asked them, 'Would you rather work in a factory or go to school?' And out of five hundred or so children, 80 percent said they would rather work in a factory

than go to school. That says something really dismal about what schools were like at that time." Historian Nancy Hoffman recalls what her mother told her about schools when she was a girl:

"You Are an American"

75

"School buildings were dangerous places. They were dark, they were drafty, they were cold. I remember my mother telling me that, as a teacher of immigrants, she got diphtheria, she got scarlet fever, and she had to deal with children who were very ill themselves and who did not have appropriate medical care."

Progressive reformers led a campaign for change. They lobbied for the enforcement of state laws that banned child labor and made school attendance compulsory. At the same time, they sought to improve the way classes were taught. As David Tyack explains: "The standard method of teaching in most urban schools was quite literally to 'toe the line.' That is, the children were expected to come up front and recite to the teacher and stand with their toes

Protest against child labor in New York City Labor Day Parade, May 1, 1909. Progressives called for enforcing child labor laws and making school compulsory.

lined up to the board and their hands in a particular place as they recited their lesson."

The rigid curriculum of the day was attacked in an 1899 book called *The School and Society,* by John Dewey. A philosopher at the University of Chicago, Dewey would become known as the father of progressive education. He wrote, "The educational center of gravity has been too long in the teacher, the textbook, anywhere and everywhere you please except in the immediate instincts and activities of the child himself." Historian Larry Cuban explains: "John Dewey believed that if schools were anchored in the whole child, in the social, intellectual, emotional, and physical development of a child, teaching would be different—and learning would be different and schools would be very different, hospitable places for children."

At the 1900 World's Fair in Paris, Americans proudly put their schools on display. They exhibited photographs of the new progressive techniques: children learning by doing, exercising their bodies as well as their minds, and venturing out of the classroom to explore the world of work and the wonders of nature. Back

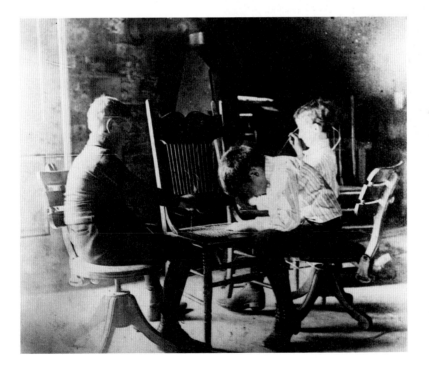

ᴀʙᴏᴠᴇ *John Dewey, 1859–1952.*

ʟᴇꜰᴛ *Children caning chairs at the Dewey Lab School in Chicago, ca. 1900.*

"You Are an American"

Schoolchildren learn with building blocks, 1899.

home, child-centered education quickly spread, even to the new industrial city of Gary, Indiana, where students got to take advantage of the most progressive school system of all.

The schools of Gary, Indiana, reflected the lofty ambitions of the town itself. In 1906, the U.S. Steel Company had built the world's largest steel mill on the shores of Lake Michigan. A city sprang up almost overnight, as immigrants flocked to Gary looking for work. To assimilate these new arrivals, town leaders hired William A. Wirt as superintendent of schools. A disciple of John Dewey, Wirt designed lavish, modern buildings that served all

LEFT

An unusual guest helps teach comparative anatomy, 1899.

BELOW

Children's circle game, 1899.

ABOVE *Exercising their bodies as well as their minds. Stretching in class, 1899.*

RIGHT *Children learn by doing. Machine shop class, 1899.*

FACING *Girls on a field trip to the museum, 1899.*

ABOVE *Venturing out of the classroom to explore the wonders of nature, 1899.*

FACING TOP *Western High School girls' exercise class, Washington, DC, 1899.*

FACING BOTTOM *"The Emerson School had at least two city blocks for territory.
Large athletic fields. A beautiful playground area, and one of the things that I remember
there was visiting their zoo. I can remember bears but nothing bigger than that."
—Marie Edwards, former student and teacher in Gary, Indiana*

"Educators embraced the idea that the college-bound program was only for the very smart kids, and that everybody else should be divided up and given a different kind of program depending on where they were expected to be in their life. So many girls were put into a household arts curriculum, many of the boys were put into an industrial education program because it was assumed that they would be factory workers. Many others were put into a commercial program because they would be clerks." —Diane Ravitch, historian

"At Horace Mann, where I went to school, in front of our campus at the main entrance, there was a beautiful lagoon, and the swans were always out there swimming." —Marie Edwards

"It was lovely to go to school. We enjoyed it!"
—Hylda Burton, former student and teacher in Gary, Indiana

grades and developed a curriculum that kept students in motion. "At first it was a little frightening because I had never been in a school where you moved from class to class at the end of each hour," says teacher Hylda Burton, a former student in Gary. "And I got lost a couple of times." Historian Ronald Cohen explains: "Wirt wanted the kids to be running around the schoolhouse, and not have them sit bored in a desk for four or five hours a day listening to the teacher drone on. What he wanted was for the kids to have a rich school experience so they were busy all the time and were getting involved in things that would interest them." Hylda Burton remembers, "They had so many things. They had a forge, and they had auto mechanics. There were all kinds of possibilities. Oh, another one was animal husbandry. The children learned how to take care of chickens and ducks. We had art classes, we had nature classes . . . there was so much going on besides our regular classroom work that it was really lovely to go to school. We enjoyed it."

All of this was possible and even affordable because of Wirt's split-shift system. In the Gary schools, every space from classroom to workshop, from auditorium to playground was in constant use. Wirt called his system Work-Study-Play. Historian

LEFT *Schools expanded their role well beyond the three Rs. Toothbrush drill, New York City, 1920.*

BELOW *Fresh-air class, P.S. 51, New York City, ca. 1911. Open-air schools were often used for children suffering from tuberculosis.*

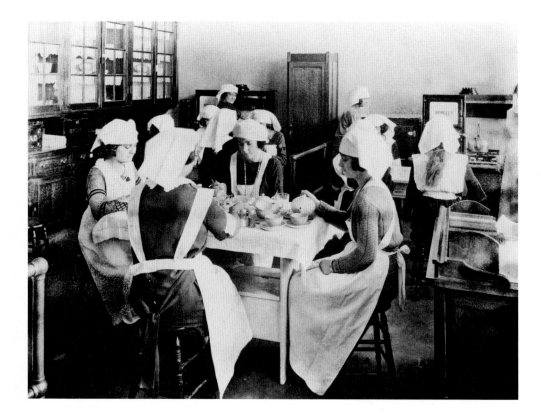

Serving tea at the Staten Island Continuation School, 1923.

David Tyack notes the diverse skills encouraged by this system. "There are many ways that young people learn. And those in the past who have been rewarded are those who are very verbal or very mathematical and could learn to spell and do their times tables efficiently. But that left behind a lot of students who had other talents, and who could contribute those talents to school. Progressive education at its best I think has been designed to tap all the talents of the student as opposed to just a narrow band."

Gary students helped to run their schools, from the printshop to the cafeteria. The goal of this manual training, a progressive ed-

School: 1900–1950

ucator said, was to "make every working man a scholar and every scholar a working man." Former student Marie Edwards says, "In the cafeteria you helped in the mass production of food. I can remember spending a week taking the eyes out of the potatoes. I got a C for talking too much while doing it, but through those two years in the junior high I came to have a pretty good idea of the whole cafeteria function and respect for the people who worked there."

In the face of massive immigration, progressives claimed that schools could help to preserve the American way of life. The new

"We were Americanized."
—Hylda Burton, former student and teacher in Gary, Indiana

"You Are an American"

Gary curriculum reached into areas like health and hygiene that had little to do with the three Rs. "These were poor people," Ronald Cohen says. "They didn't have indoor plumbing in Gary, they didn't have sanitary facilities . . . so you brought the kids into the school where you cleaned them up. Part of the reason they had swimming pools in the school was so kids would have a bath. So the school was there to do everything the parents were not doing." Hylda Burton, whose family immigrated to Gary, describes being taught manners in school: "The vice principal would put on an afternoon tea to just show us how we would behave. She would show us such things as a bath mat, which I had never seen before in my life (I thought it was a towel) and she explained what it was. She

Saluting the flag in the Mott Street Industrial School, New York, ca. 1898.

School: 1900–1950

would teach us manners that we used here. We had fifty-three nationalities in Froebel School. And we were Americanized."

The Gary schools were open at night and on weekends to serve the entire community. Leaders of industry hoped that progressive education would socialize students and their families at a time of widespread labor unrest. "The argument is made that the reason there are labor riots and strikes is because the family can't manage their budget," explains Joel Spring. "So home economics become a big issue. If the woman learns how to cook and the worker goes to work well fed and works hard, and knows that there will be a good meal when he returns home, he doesn't stop at the saloon and he comes directly home. And we will have industrial peace through home economics. So the school was suddenly the panacea for everything that was going on in society."

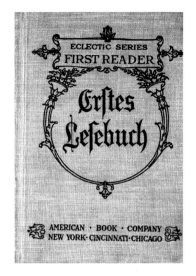

Erstes Lesebuch
(First Reader),
*one of many
German-language
textbooks used in
American public
schools prior
to World War I.*

The schools of Gary drew visitors from as far away as Japan. Eventually, educators from two hundred American cities adopted Wirt's system. In New York, progressive mayor John Mitchel put the "Gary Plan" into action in thirty New York schools. But that move embroiled the school system, and the city, in a violent controversy. In the mayor's race of 1917, Democratic opponent John Hylan attacked the Gary Plan as a plot to turn out cheap labor for large corporations: "I say to you, Mr. Mayor, hands off our public schools. Our boys and girls shall have an opportunity to become

lawyers, doctors, clergymen, musicians, poets or men of letters, notwithstanding the views of the Board of Education!" At a time when nearly 70 percent of New York students were from immigrant families, Hylan's words struck a nerve. As historian Diane Ravitch explains, "Most of the immigrants were from eastern Europe, many of them were Jewish, and they wanted their children to get the best possible academic education. They didn't want their kids to be prepared to work in a factory, which is the way they perceived the Gary Plan." Tensions built into riots that

The attitude toward immigrants shifted with the outbreak of World War I.

broke out a week before the mayoral election. Crowds of five thousand people broke school windows, overturned cars, and stoned policemen. One immigrant mother in Brooklyn protested, "We want our Kinder to learn mit der book, der paper, und der pencil,

School: 1900–1950

not mit der sewing and der shop! Dey are unserer Kinder, not theirs!"

John Hylan won the 1917 mayor's race by a landslide, and announced the end of the Gary Plan in New York. The city's schools returned to the more traditional curriculum in use earlier in the century. Still, as in Gary, educators faced the task of socializing large numbers of immigrant children. New York published its own series of textbooks that focused on the English language, patriotism, and American citizenship. Alfred Kazin remembers, "Officially the idea was to get us out of the barbarism of our immigrant

Christian holidays were part of the curriculum even in New York City, where large numbers of students were Jewish. Photo ca. 1900.

"You Are an American"

93

Pietro learning to write, Jersey Street. Southern Italians were the second largest immigrant group in New York City schools in the 1920s.

background but the idea was 'to Americanize us,' as they say, and it did." Historian Nancy Hoffman notes that all of the teaching took place in English. "Classes were of mixed age, something that we think about as controversial today," she says, "and [they] were often filled with students who spoke eight or ten or fifteen different languages.... There was certainly just a sink or swim situation." Bel Kaufman, author of *Up the Down Staircase*, remembers, "At twelve I was placed in the first grade with all the little children half my age . . . in one of those funny little desks that were attached to the floor and I remember my knees up to my chin.... Now I had to leave the room, I didn't know what to say. So I listened. I thought I got it. I waved a frantic hand and I said,

School: 1900–1950

'Moooromm,' and the teacher understood. I later found out that it was 'May I leave the room?'"

New York's English-only curriculum was radical for its day. In the years before World War I, schools in many cities had taught courses in the language of the major immigrant group, such as German. David Tyack explains, "The Germans came to this country and were quite proud of their own language and tradition and insisted that their language be taught in places like St. Louis and Cincinnati and Cleveland. Hundreds of thousands of children learned German or learned in German in public schools.

1923 honor roll certificate of Bella Kaufman. "Bel" Kaufman worked as a teacher in the New York public schools. Her book Up the Down Staircase *was based on her experiences.*

And learned about the glories of Germany." But by 1917, the United States was at war. Former president Theodore Roosevelt was among those leading the call for an English-only curriculum. "We have room for but one language here, and that is the English language," he wrote. "For we intend to see that the crucible turns our people out as Americans, of American nationality, and not as dwellers of a polyglot boardinghouse." The movement took hold after the Allied victory in 1918. Soon, thirty-five states required instruction in English only, and schools emphasized American heroes and anthems. Russian-born Bel Kaufman remembers, "I looked up in the dictionary under 'V' a word that was verspacious. I knew it was a color word, vermillion was red, verspacious must be blue. I couldn't find it. Yet every Friday in assembly we sang 'Oh beautiful verspacious skies.'"

Many schools also required that students recite passages from the Bible, or the Lord's Prayer. Christian holidays were celebrated, even in cities like New York, where large numbers of students were Jewish. To young immigrants, even the secular holidays were foreign. "Thanksgiving was unknown at home, it was hardly one of the Jewish holidays," says Alfred Kazin. "Nevertheless Thanksgiving at school became something terrific. We would have to cut out little figures of Pilgrims and with a nasty white paste that we made ourselves, we put these on the windows of the school. On the other hand, it would never have occurred to us to bring our holidays into the schoolroom, so that there was a compromise."

Crossing the cultural divide between home and school could be even harder for southern Italians, New York's second largest immigrant group. They came mostly from rural backgrounds, and in the 1920s, two-thirds of their children left school by the eighth grade. "The good child was the child who went to the docks with the father when he turned fifteen, and helped bring money home for the family," explains David Tyack. "And the bad child was the one who wanted to hang out in school and play baseball, and thought high school was just great, and so there was very little reinforcement for achieving in school and a lot of reinforcement for helping out at home." Still, growing numbers of immigrants na-

School: 1900–1950

tionwide saw education as the ticket to the best America had to offer.

By the 1920s, the nation seemed to be rushing forward, as fast as automobiles could roll off Henry Ford's assembly line, as fast as women in the steno pool could type *The Quick Brown Fox*. America's schools, too, were moving ahead. In 1920, $1 billion was spent on public education, and 17 percent of seventeen-year-olds graduated from high school. Since the turn of the century, new high schools had been opening at the rate of one per day. Now there were kindergartens for five-year-olds and junior highs for adolescents. As the system expanded, so did the bureaucracy. Chester Finn, assistant secretary for the Department of Education under President Ronald Reagan, explains: "You add a library, you need a chief librarian, you start providing lunch, you need somebody in charge of food services, if you start providing transportation, you'll need somebody in charge of transportation. Instead of having just teachers, you suddenly have separate math and science teachers, well, then you have to have a department of math teachers, and you have a chairman for math teachers and a supervisor of math teachers. So the more complex the organization, the more bureaucratized it gets. And bureaucracy begets itself."

Enter a new generation of progressive educators, now steeped in the cult of efficiency. Ellwood P. Cubberley had started out as a teacher in a one-room Indiana schoolhouse, which offered a single curriculum to all students. Cubberley came to regard this "one

size fits all" education as woefully out of date. "We should give up the exceedingly democratic idea that all are equal and that our society is devoid of classes. The employee tends to remain an employee; the wage earner tends to remain a wage earner.... One bright child may easily be worth more to the National Life than thousands of those of low mentality." As head of the Department of Education at Stanford University, Cubberley trained a generation of administrators in what was called the "science" of school management. Instead of offering all students the same classical, college-prep curriculum, high schools now "tracked" students into an array of educational paths. "Peo-

tracking

School: 1900–1950

ple began to think of going to school as a way of getting a job, not going to school to become a wise person or . . . a consumer of literature," says Joel Spring. "And in fact, [educators] asked the question 'Does a bricklayer really need to know Shakespeare?' They decided that only those who are going on to college should study Shakespeare, and bricklayers would receive a different type of English to study."

Tracking seemed an efficient way to sort through growing numbers of students. To determine placement, school administrators

Traditionally, high schools had given everyone the same college-preparatory curriculum.

turned to a test designed to measure what was called a student's intelligence quotient, or **I.Q.** Developed in France, I.Q. tests were popularized by psychologist Lewis Terman, a colleague of Cubberley's at Stanford University. "Lewis Terman believed that the intelligence test was a technology that could transform America and help it achieve a Utopia," says Paul Chapman, a biographer of Terman. "In Terman's view, if we could use the test to assess every child in the public schools, we would have a better understanding of each individual's ability or capacity, and create a kind of social efficiency for the country."

Earlier, during World War I, Terman and a group of psychologists had field-tested their exam on 1.7 million U.S. Army recruits. Scores on word and picture problems helped to determine which men would be assigned desk jobs in Washington, and which men would be sent to the trenches in France. Psychologists concluded, based on I.Q. tests, that the average mental age of American adults was 13.7 years and that ethnicity affected intelligence. These controversial theories, later disproved, would have a major impact on schoolchildren nationwide. "There was this sense that **I.Q.** tests could be used to determine the quality of people by ethnicity, by race, by class," says historian James Anderson. "And so the very belief in the capacity of people to learn was undermined, particularly by psychologists like Terman."

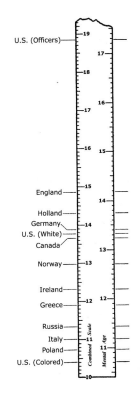

FACING *"Complete the Picture." World War I Army Beta (I.Q.) test, 1918.*

ABOVE *"Mental ages" of racial and ethnic groups based on I.Q. tests given to World War I recruits.*

"You Are an American"

By the 1920s, over a million children were undergoing I.Q. tests each year. Questions were designed to measure mental aptitude rather than academic achievement, and could be highly subjective. The International Intelligence Test of 1927, for example, asks: "TRUE OR FALSE: We seldom desire food when we are sad. TRUE OR FALSE: A large man is always braver than a small one." Yet the tests inspired trust. "Terman had a great flair for dealing with school districts, for dealing with the media," says author Nicholas Lemann. "He had this project where he derived the I.Q.s of famous figures throughout history, which is scientifically a complete crock. But it got huge pickup in the media and really helped to popularize the idea of I.Q. as the crucial human quality." By Terman's estimate, Copernicus had an I.Q. of 130; Leonardo da Vinci, 150; George Washington, 135; Immanuel Kant, 145; Beethoven, 140; Abraham Lincoln, 140; and Thomas Jefferson, 150.

In the early 1800s, Thomas Jefferson had called upon schools to "rake the best geniuses from the rubbish." In the 1920s, the Los Angeles schools were using I.Q. tests to spot future leaders. They found Russell Robinson, whose score of 145 put him in the top half of 1 percent of all American students. As he remembers, "I found school very easy. I liked some subjects particularly— physics and chemistry and mathematics. I don't remember being good at English and I don't think I liked history but I took all the shop courses that were given." Robinson graduated from Santa

Monica High School at the ripe age of fifteen, and earned a scholarship to Stanford University. At the time, belief in the power of testing extended beyond I.Q. measurement to aptitude in everything from home economics skills to citizenship, in what one critic called "an orgy of tabulation." At Stanford, Robinson had to take a vocational interest test, even though he was already an engineering student. "The conclusion was that I would make an excellent YMCA secretary but a mediocre engineer. I think my career proved that I was a little more than mediocre." Robinson became, literally, a rocket scientist, whose forty-year career at the National Aeronautics and Space Administration established him as one of the nation's top aerodynamic engineers.

With the Great Depression of the 1930s, widespread unemployment kept even more children in school. A federal law was finally passed that banned child labor, and all states required school attendance, at least until age sixteen. Faced with hard times and crowded schools, educators increasingly used the I.Q. tests to track students. The results continue to draw criticism. "If you are a person who gets high I.Q. test scores, very high, in the top 1 percent, America will find you," says Nicholas Lemann. "They will come to your door, they will give you a scholarship and they will put you on the road to success. That is very good for those people. But the trouble with the I.Q. movement, among many troubles, is that there is a tendency to write off everybody else." Adding further complication, the tests were generally given in English.

"You Are an American"

Henry Nava, whose parents emigrated from Mexico to Los Angeles, recalls taking the tests as a child, but not knowing why. "I remember being given a few tests but I was never told what the purpose was. We thought they were some type of analysis of students or something." His brother Julian adds, "I remember just being tracked into shop courses, so I guess I didn't test very well." "They believe you can start testing for I.Q. at about age five," says Nicholas Lemann. "And that at age ten the score stabilizes for life. They also believe that although most I.Q. tests are longer, about twelve minutes will do it. The really favorite items of the I.Q. testers are antonyms, synonyms, and analogies. And those are very heavily dependent on what kind of house you grew up in." Says Henry Nava, "Our father was a barber and quite well self-educated. So he started telling us about the value of reading and getting an education. Our mother was a school teacher in her small town in Mexico." Julian adds, "My mother didn't learn English. We spoke only Spanish at home." Historian Gilbert Gonzalez comments, "It must have been a heavy burden for children entering kindergarten or the first grade to be given a test possibly in a language they didn't understand. This test would become for them really a mark that they would have to carry for the rest of their lives."

By the 1930s, two-thirds of the Mexican American students in Los Angeles were classified as slow learners, and even mentally retarded, on the basis of I.Q. tests given as early as kindergarten. "We were held back," declares Julian Nava. "Not because

School: 1900–1950

Mexican American students in Bridge Street Elementary School, Los Angeles, 1931.

someone hated us, but because the teachers accepted who we were on the basis of our family and heritage, and kind of assumed that we would repeat the pattern of our parents and so they were helping us get ready for the future." In 1941, Julian followed his older brother Henry into Roosevelt High School. Like other Mexican American students, they were shunted toward vocational courses such as auto mechanics and carpentry. Henry describes being prevented from studying subjects he wanted to take. "I expressed interest in some college prep classes. But they just said, well, they are kind of hard. We don't know if you want to concentrate or study that hard because you are doing so well in wood shop and you should develop that skill."

During World War II, twenty-year-old Henry Nava joined the Navy Medical Corps and shipped out to the Pacific. He quickly noticed that servicemen with lower levels of education were assigned to the most hazardous duty. "That is when I started realizing the greater value of some education," he says with a smile, "and I started trying to tell my brother about it." His younger brother Julian adds, "He saw many injured people in Hawaii, troops that were coming back with serious injuries and he didn't want to have me go through that experience." While home on leave, Henry took Julian to see the high school guidance counselor. "Henry insisted that I be allowed to take college prep courses and faced refusal," Julian continues. "I remember that Henry was a weight lifter and Navy uniforms are very tight fitting and so he had very broad shoulders and big biceps, and he looked

Julian Nava (seated on chair in center, front row) with class outside Roosevelt High School, Los Angeles, ca. 1945.

Many Mexican American students were shunted into vocational courses such as wood shop.

just awesome in his Navy uniform. And he leaned over on the desk and he told the counselor, 'You didn't hear me. Julian is going to take college prep courses.' And [to me] he said, 'And you are going to pass these, aren't you?' And I said yes. A good Mexican boy always says 'yes' to his older brother."

Julian Nava graduated from high school in 1945 and went on to earn a doctorate in history from Harvard University. He was later elected to the Los Angeles Board of Education, and in 1979 was

School: 1900–1950

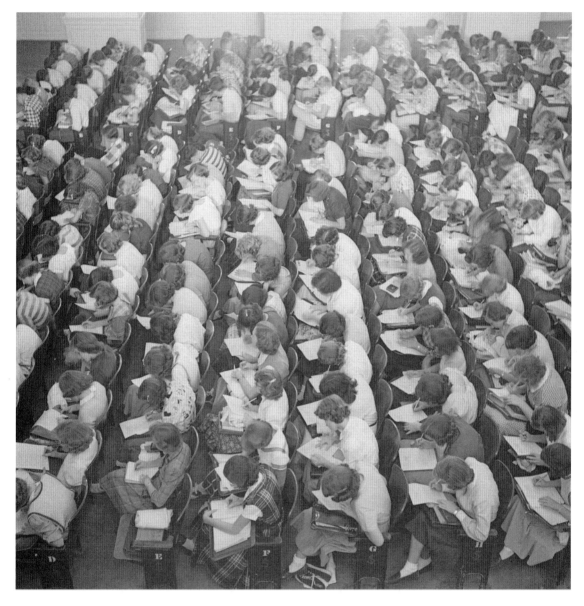

The SAT, cousin of the I.Q. test, became the gateway to higher education after World War II.

named U.S. ambassador to Mexico by President Jimmy Carter. Nava's success defied the educational odds faced by many minority students. "One of the things that is standard practice during this time is to assume that Mexican children were not going to be able to compete with Anglo American children, and therefore they needed to be segregated," explains Gilbert Gonzalez. "Some districts didn't even require intelligence tests—they just created the Mexican school as an industrial school, assuming that this is the kind of work that they were capable of doing."

Industrial training also dominated the curriculum at Native American boarding schools run by the federal government. "The emphasis was upon taking away people's culture and replacing it with the dominant white Anglo-Saxon culture of the United States," says Joel Spring. "An important part of that was getting rid of Native American languages. They wanted people to learn English and English only. So there was a belief that they were bringing people into the mainstream of American values, and at the same time preparing them to enter the labor market."

African American children, in segregated schools in the South, also faced restrictions. African American girls were taught domestic science, and boys learned to work with their hands. "When you look at the curricula that was developed—domestic science for women, industrial education for African Americans, boarding schools for Native Americans—much of what developed under the guise of a democratic and differentiated curriculum was in fact a way to reinforce the kind of class, gender, and race prejudice that existed in society," explains historian James Anderson. Julian Nava agrees: "It has been an enormous loss to our country. We will never know how many Doctor Salks or Pablo Casals or Picassos have been lost because children from minority groups were not inspired or challenged and given the chance to show what they've got."

In the 1960s and 1970s, Julian Nava led a successful fight to ban I.Q. testing in the Los Angeles schools. Other minority leaders helped to end career tracking in the schools of Washington, D.C. Yet millions of students in the United States continued to be evaluated by the I.Q. test and its newer cousin, the Scholastic Aptitude Test, or S.A.T. Testing and tracking remain controversial to this day.

At mid-century, more American students were graduating than ever before. In 1900, 6 percent of seventeen-year-olds were high school graduates. By 1945, that number had risen to 51 percent, and bobby-soxers were making school the center of their social lives. More students meant a wider range of abilities, posing problems for educators. Historian Joel Spring explains: "What do we do with the 60 percent of students who are not gaining anything from a college-preparatory curriculum or a vocational curriculum? The answer that was given by educators was, we will give them 'life adjustment education.'" Created by the U.S. Office of Education, the life adjustment movement sought to extend

Health and hygiene lesson, ca. 1950s.

[handwritten: try to make curriculum relevant]

progressive education by making school relevant to teenagers' daily lives. Taking advantage of the latest audiovisual aids, life adjustment taught practical lessons in family life, hygiene, and health. Once again, schools were expanding their reach beyond the three Rs.

Life adjustment was not progressive education as John Dewey had envisioned it. Yet prominent critics blasted the entire movement. Progressive education was REgressive education, according to postwar critic Arthur Bestor. "The West was not settled by

School: 1900–1950

114

men and women who had taken a course in 'How to Be a Pioneer.' I for one do not believe that the American people have lost all common sense and native wit so that they now have to be taught in school to blow their nose and button their pants." In his 1953 best-seller, *Educational Wastelands,* Bestor drew on his observations as a university professor and as a parent of children in the public schools. His son Theodore remembers, "He would sometimes look at my social studies textbooks and feel that they were inadequate because lots of things were being spoon-fed to students. They weren't forced to think through this set of information, analyze it in some framework, evaluate the data and come to conclusions."

Charging that schools had gotten badly off track, Bestor led a campaign for a return to basic academic subjects. Historian David Tyack explains: "Critics of American education argued that it had been downhill ever since the progressives started adding on course after course to what had been a more traditional curriculum." At the same time, Tyack notes, "If you have ever spent the entire day sitting—as students do—in a math class, and an English class, and a history class, and then go to the shop class or go to the art class or go to the music class, you realize how this kind of variety enhances school and enhances the kinds of skills and knowledge and relationships that students need to take away from school." Still, the criticism had an effect, says historian Larry Cuban. "Post–World War II critics like Arthur Bestor strengthened the return of traditional schools that John Dewey himself

"You Are an American"

Cover of LIFE *magazine in 1958, published the year after* Sputnik, *graphically compared American students to those in the Soviet Union.*

had railed against at the beginning of the twentieth century. And
so you have this cyclical kind of movement between progressive
and traditional kinds of teaching, learning and schooling that has
gone on in American schools for almost a century." Theodore Bestor describes the political climate that lay behind his father's
zeal: "My father was writing during the height of the McCarthy
era. And I think he was very much committed to the idea that the
American political system requires an educated, articulate, intel-
ligent citizenry. And that if the schools don't provide people with
the tools for doing that, what will become of us?"

"You Are an American"

In Cold War America, tolerance for progressive ideals was waning. Progressive textbooks that discussed socialism and communism were attacked by right-wing groups as un-American. As fears of a nuclear war gripped the country, schools held civil defense drills to prepare children for an enemy attack. Amid this Cold War paranoia, it was only fitting that the question of what schools should teach would be settled by a rocket—a Soviet rocket. Chester Finn describes the effect of the Soviet Union's successful launch of *Sputnik* in October 1957: "Suddenly they were in outer space before we were. And how could this have happened? How could they have gotten the jump on us scientifically and technologically? And the immediate assumption, rightly or wrongly, was that they must be better educated."

In 1958, President Dwight Eisenhower signed the National Defense Education Act. For the first time, massive amounts of federal money—over $100 million annually—were sent to aid public education. Overnight, the schools changed. Joel Spring recalls the effect of *Sputnik* on his math class: "A teacher in my classroom pointed her finger at me and said, 'There is Ivan in the Soviet Union studying math and you are studying math and if you don't do well, we are going to lose to communism.' And I was forced out of history courses into math and physics programs as a result of *Sputnik*." University scholars designed high-level math and science courses. Advanced students went into training as future engineers and astronauts.

Early in the century, public schools had opened up a world of promise for children who came off steamships and out of factories and farms. In the decades that followed, schools offered some children job training and groomed others for future leadership. The legacy of this era was a system of mass education, but one that educated different groups differently. The goal for the next generation would be to ensure equal education for *all* of America's children.

Part Three

1950-1980

SEPARATE
AND
UNEQUAL

Introduction

JAMES D. ANDERSON

In a wonderful book about history and memory, Richard White reminds us that any good history begins in strangeness. "The past should be so strange that you wonder how you and people you know and love could come from such a time."[1] As we advance in the modern crusade for equal educational opportunity, we realize that its form and content in 1950 varied considerably from that of the present. America in 1950 was a fundamentally different nation, one that is increasingly difficult to comprehend and appreciate from our contemporary angle of vision. In 1950, though it was often dangerous—and in seventeen states illegal—for ethnic minorities to attend so-called white public schools, the promise of American public education held a special place in the hearts and minds of citizens across the nation. From the viewpoints of various minority communities, public schooling affected their children's chances for active participation in American life and served as the main community issue

1. Richard White, *Remembering Ahanagran: Storytelling in a Family's Past* (New York: Hill & Wang, 1998), 13.

around which different people could rally to promote achievement, equality, and the promise of the American dream. As the experience of the past five decades has brought with it consequences not imagined in 1950, goals and struggles that once seemed noble are now faded dreams and points of contention. Discussions of school integration, for example, have been removed from the national agenda and find expression only in lawsuits and isolated corners of academics. Since the formative stages of the civil rights movement, the role of public education in a democracy has been constantly redefined. Hence, a dialogue between the past and the present on the critical issues raised by *Brown v. Board of Education* and the resulting campaigns for equal educational opportunity seems much needed at this moment in the nation's history.

To be sure, the opportunity to achieve a good education and the right to attend school without discrimination are still valued in most American communities. Though the issue of equal educational opportunity remains serious business, virtually no one today thinks of it as an issue that one might have to die for. This was not so five decades ago. In 1950, people had to risk their lives and futures for equal educational opportunities. When Joseph Albert Delaine filed a lawsuit against local white school officials for not providing school buses for his three children, he understood that the consequences could be fatal. Local white authorities in Clarendon County, South Carolina, home of one of the five consolidated cases that we now know as *Brown v. Board of Education,* fired him from the little schoolhouse where he had taught for ten years. They also fired his wife, two of his sisters, and a niece. Then they burned his house to the ground. They stoned the church at which he pastored and fired shotguns at him out of the dark. Ultimately they burned down his church and ran him from the state.[2]

Melba Pattillo Beals, one of the nine African American teenagers chosen in 1957 to integrate Little Rock's Central High School, began her memoir with a statement of gratitude that makes sense only in the context of the violent confrontations that characterized the mid-century struggles for educational equality. "I will always be grateful to the men of the 101st Airborne, who did

2. Richard Kluger, *Simple Justice: The History of Brown v. Board of Education and Black America's Struggle for Equality* (New York: Knopf, 1976), 3.

their personal best to protect us from attacks."[3] In 1957, while white teenage girls were listening to Buddy Holly's "Peggy Sue," Melba Pattillo Beals was escaping the hanging rope of a lynch mob, dodging lighted sticks of dynamite, and washing away burning acid sprayed into her eyes. To uphold the law and protect the lives of students, President Dwight David Eisenhower sent the 101st Airborne Division, the elite "Screaming Eagles," to Little Rock to keep the doors of Central High open and allow the nine teenagers to complete a full day of classes. At the center of the controversy were nine African American young people who wanted a better education. Although most attempts to attain a better education were not attended by such extreme violence, the campaigns of terrorism that included telephone threats, insults and assaults at school, brigades of attacking white citizens, rogue police, and economic blackmail were characteristic of the 1950s and 1960s.

For example, on September 3, 1965, seven of Mae Bertha and Matthew Carter's children lined up to wait for the school bus that would take them to desegregate the all-white public schools in Sunflower County, Mississippi. Soon after their successful attempts to desegregate the all-white Drew High School, the Carters' home was riddled with bullets in the middle of the night. The owner of the plantation on which they lived canceled their credit at his store and threw them off his land. At school the Carter children were tormented by white students and by some of the teachers. The Carters understood that their children would endure physical and psychological punishment in the hostile racial climate of their new school. Still, they felt that changing schools was their best chance to get their children out of the cotton fields. Eight Carter children graduated from Drew High School, and seven went on to college at the University of Mississippi.[4]

Melba Pattillo Beals closes her memoir with a statement that compels us to revisit the 1950s with a sense of strangeness and unfamiliarity. "As I watch videotapes now and think back to that first day at Central High on September 4, 1957, I wonder what possessed my parents and the adults of the NAACP to

3. Melba Pattillo Beals, *Warriors Don't Cry: A Searing Memoir of the Battle to Integrate Little Rock's Central High* (New York: Pocket Books, 1994), 4.

4. Constance Curry, *Silver Rights* (Chapel Hill, NC: Algonquin Books, 1995).

allow us to go to that school in the face of such violence."[5] Beals raises questions that should remain a part of our ongoing debate about the meaning of public education in American democracy. Why were parents and ordinary citizens willing to face injury and death to achieve superior educational opportunities? Why were white Southerners ready to inflict great harm to exclude African Americans? Grappling with such questions is a formidable task, and it has much to do with the relationships between minority groups and the larger transformation of American education and democracy at mid-century.

In the larger society of 1950, public schooling was a central part of American culture and was perceived by parents as vital to their children's future. The transformation of public secondary education during the first third of the twentieth century symbolized the extent to which schooling had become a strategic part of the national experience in 1950. From about 1890 to 1935, the American high school was transformed from an elite, private institution into a public one attended by white children en masse. Educational opportunities were expanding; publicly and privately supported schemes to locate the talented burgeoned, and scholarship and loan programs for those students were provided with equal enthusiasm. Minorities knew they were being cheated of access to the new educational opportunities. As the public high school, only a marginal factor in American life at the dawn of the twentieth century, became the "people's college" by mid-century, such exclusion reflected the larger system of racial subordination.[6]

African Americans, Latinos, and Native Americans in particular were virtually excluded from this important transformation. For example, whereas 54 percent of southern white children of high school age were enrolled in public high schools by 1935, more than eight out of every ten African American children of high school age were not enrolled in secondary schools. As late as 1968, the average schooling for Mexican Americans in Texas was 4.7 years.

By 1950, the inequality in educational achievement between white students and minority students had deepened since 1900, when very few Americans of

5. Beals, *Warriors Don't Cry*, 5.

6. James D. Anderson, *The Education of Blacks in the South, 1860–1935* (Chapel Hill: University of North Carolina Press, 1988), 187.

School: 1950–1980

any race or gender attended high schools, and formal education was only marginally a factor in national economic and social life. As ethnic minority groups and women sensed a growing gap in educational opportunities, campaigns to provide better educational opportunities for their children became a critical social issue and a central plank in the larger platform for civil and political equality. Lacking access, for the most part, to voting power, political offices, finance, and the higher reaches of industry, parents, community leaders, and ordinary citizens focused on the right to equal educational opportunity as the centerpiece of the larger crusade for justice and equality. As Melba Pattillo Beals recalled, "Back then, I naively believed that if we could end segregation in the schools, all barriers of inequality would fall. If you had asked me in 1957 what I expected, I would have told you that by this time [1994] our struggle for human rights would have been won."[7] Getting the best education possible for their children motivated ordinary citizens to show extraordinary grit, courage, and endurance, challenging Jim Crow and other legal and customary forms of racial, ethnic, gender, and disability subordination.

The crusades for equal educational opportunity that began in Topeka, Kansas, Farmville, Virginia, and Little Rock, Arkansas, spread across the nation, aiding various struggles for learning and self-improvement. In 1966, African American students at Northern High in Detroit called a general strike to protest the failure of urban schools and to demand better educational opportunities. Mexican American high school students in Crystal City, Texas, went on strike in 1968, demanding bilingual education, more humane treatment from white teachers, and curricular reform to include the history and culture of Mexicans in the Southwest. Similarly, in the fall of 1968, approximately thirty thousand African American and Latino students embarked on a sustained boycott to protest the quality of education provided by the schools as well as the treatment accorded students by white teachers, counselors, and administrators. Their proposals for school reform included a demand for community participation in school programs, more African American and Latino school administrators, African American and Latino history courses, and more homework for stu-

7. Beals, *Warriors Don't Cry*, 3.

dents. Minority students were demanding excellence in education long before politicians used it as a political football in the 1980s.

The grassroots school reform movements of the 1960s spilled into the 1970s and expanded among different minority populations. The movement for instruction in a language other than English received a boost from the U.S. Supreme Court when Chinese Americans in California sued successfully for ESL (English as a Second Language) programs. Feminist leaders pushed for laws and programs to give female students educational equality. In 1972, the U.S. Congress passed Title IX, which prohibited the awarding of federal grants to programs that discriminated on the basis of gender. In 1976, the crusade for equal educational opportunity embraced children with disabilities. As with racial integration, bilingual education, and Title IX, the movement to provide resources and training to make learning possible for children with disabilities challenged the simple beliefs and uniform rules about public education and democracy embodied in the dominant culture at mid-century.

From our contemporary angle of vision, perceptions are sharply conflicting about what has happened in communities where equal educational plans have been implemented. Instead of bringing about better race/ethnic and gender relations and improved academic performance, many conservatives argue, the historic Brown decision and the resulting campaigns for equality have heightened gender and racial tensions, fostered white flight from urban school districts, and caused a general deterioration in standards of behavior and schoolwork. Conservatives maintain that the harm to public education has been so great that the attempt to integrate the nation's schools has been a tragic failure. From this viewpoint, the crusade for equal educational opportunity is defined as a burden, a social policy to force into schools preconceived notions about racial and gender equality at the expense of academic excellence. President Ronald Reagan's campaign for "Excellence in Education" counterpoised excellence as virtually the opposite of equality. Educators and scholars began to debate whether the nation could have both equality and excellence.

Clearly these thinkers did not fully understand or appreciate why sixteen-year-old Barbara Johns led the student strike at Moton High School in Farmville, Virginia, in 1951 or why Mae Bertha and Matthew Carter encouraged their children to risk physical and psychological punishment in pursuit of a better

School: 1950–1980

education. Further, they seem to have no memory of the students in Chicago and Detroit who went on strike in the 1960s demanding more homework and advanced-placement courses while decrying the practice of social promotion. Was this not a demand for academic excellence? The pursuit of academic excellence and the demand for first-rate educational facilities were the underlying causes of the crusade for equal educational opportunity, not the pursuit of liberal social policies for their intrinsic value. Moreover, the demand for academic excellence and better educational opportunities by various minority communities predated by several decades the "Excellence in Education" campaign of the 1980s. How conservatives and neoconservatives could become so disconnected from the core values of the crusade for equal educational opportunities underscores the need for a national conversation about education and democracy in the twenty-first century.

Some members of minority communities became increasingly disenchanted with the results of the crusade for equal educational opportunity. Minority leaders brought to the campaign different cultural values and different political assumptions. Most, of course, were related to power and control over education, since they had come to view white control as the essence of racial subordination and segregation. Many minorities wanted desegregation to be a process of sharing power and control over education. They resisted attempts by local school boards to close schools located in their communities and force minority students to be bused to the formerly all white schools. They wanted assurances that minority principals, teachers, and service workers would not lose their jobs during school desegregation. They also wanted some community control over, and participation in, curricular programs. Finally, they wanted promises that minority students would not be "tracked" into lower-level classes, a process that amounted to racial segregation and subordination within "desegregated" schools.

Hence, minority group leaders viewed the school desegregation process as an opportunity to gain some power and control over local educational systems and to end their long-standing subordination within the educational system. Over the past five decades, ethnic, minority, and feminist campaigns for equal educational opportunity have challenged and redefined the simple, dominant beliefs about democracy and education that characterized America at mid-century. The theory of democracy and education that then prevailed was informed by conceptions of social homogeneity, simplicity, and an overarching common identity of whiteness, rather than social diversity, complexity, and multiple identities. Most Americans in 1950 grew up with the idealized model of the town meeting, where people from similar backgrounds came together to debate the common good within parameters so narrow as to virtually exclude women, African Americans, Latinos, and Asian Americans. The heterogeneous civil rights struggles of the past decades have significantly challenged this conception of democracy. What we now face are cultural, political, educational, and legal debates over the extent to which our democracy can or ought to absorb heterogeneity and cultural pluralism. In the face of increasing diversity, a simple, homogeneous model of democracy and education will fail. Young Americans need to learn how to accept diversity, negotiate conflicts, and form coalitions if they are to be leaders in an increasingly heterogeneous and complex society. One of the long-term contributions of the recent struggles for educational equality may be the shift in our understanding of the role of public schooling in a diverse democracy.[8]

In 1954, Edwin R. Murrow devoted an entire half hour of his CBS television program *See It Now* to an effort to understand attitudes toward the *Brown* decision of certain persons in Gastonia, North Carolina, and Nachitoches, Louisiana. An African American boy in Nachitoches said of the decision, "I think it's the wonderfullest thing that's ever happened to America." The choices that we now make regarding public education will determine the wisdom of his opinion.

8. Grace Elizabeth Hale, *Making Whiteness: The Culture of Segregation in the South, 1890–1940* (New York: Pantheon Books, 1998).

School: 1950–1980

"Why Don't You Go to School with Us?"

We [wanted] what democracy had said was ours.
And what our Bill of Rights and our Constitution
had said belonged to us. We wanted equality, definitely.

SEVERITA LARA

Rev. Oliver Brown, plaintiff in landmark Supreme Court case Brown v. Board of Education, *with his daughter Linda and family in Topeka, Kansas.*

I n the 1950s, America's schools were bursting with the promise of a new generation, the postwar baby boomers. It was up to the schools to inoculate these children against disease—and to prepare them for a nuclear attack. Schools were also expected to propel the nation's youth toward a technological future. Three out of five students graduated in 1950, and almost 50 percent of them went on to college. Yet these gains masked profound inequalities. "The promise of the public schools from the time of Jefferson, Horace Mann, and the early proponents of common schooling was that all students were entitled to a quality education and to be educated together," says Jay Heubert, an expert on law and school reform. "In the 1950s, however, that

Fourth- and fifth-grade classes at the segregated, all-white Van Buren School in Topeka, Kansas, 1949.

simply wasn't the case." Adds Marcia Greenberger, head of the National Women's Law Center, "There were no teams in athletics for young women, no scholarships for women in athletics in college. There were many professional schools not open to women. Many of the prestigious colleges were closed to women." Jose Angel Gutierrez, a Chicano civil rights leader from Crystal City, Texas, recalls, "There was rigid segregation within the building,

School: 1950–1980

within the classrooms. In other words, English One was basically all Anglo, and English Five was basically all Mexican."

In 1950, African American students were segregated by law in seventeen states. Mexican Americans attended school an average of 5.6 years. And 72 percent of disabled school-age children were not enrolled. It took a great wave of education reform, from the 1950s through the 1970s, to open America's schools to everyone. This crusade was led by activists, parents, and students themselves. Severita Lara, former Crystal City student leader and mayor of Crystal City from 1995 to 1997, remembers, "We weren't looking to grab or get things that didn't belong to us, just what democracy had said was ours. And what our Bill of Rights and our

Fifth- and sixth-grade classes at the segregated, all-black Monroe School in Topeka, Kansas, 1949.

"Why Don't You Go to School with Us?"

Constitution had said belonged to us. . . . We wanted equality, definitely."

The modern fight for equality in the nation's schools began in Topeka, the capital of Kansas, and it hinged on the issue of race. Topeka's million-dollar high school was integrated, with African Americans and whites attending class together. Yet most school activities were segregated. Blacks and whites had separate proms, separate student governments, and, until 1950, even separate sports teams and cheerleading squads. At the elementary level, Topeka's schools were strictly segregated: there were eighteen public schools for white children, and four for African Americans. Linda Brown Thompson, daughter of the lead plaintiff in the sem-

Linda Brown's kindergarten class at the segregated Monroe School. (Linda Brown is standing in the top row, fourth from the right.)

School: 1950–1980

inal Supreme Court case *Brown v. Board of Education,* remembers what it was like to attend a segregated school. "I lived in a neighborhood that was integrated and I had playmates of all nationalities—Native Americans, Caucasians—that I played with, Hispanic children. And then when school started, we would go these opposite directions. And of course your playmates you played with every day wanted to know, 'Well, why don't you go to school with us?'"

Shut out of their neighborhood school, Linda Brown and her sister had to walk through a railroad yard to catch a bus to the all-black Monroe School, two miles from home. African American parents in Topeka had fought this discrimination for years. "They went to the school board, they talked to the school board, they did everything that they could in order to get them to understand, hey, our kids are deserving of the same type of education that you are giving to everybody else," recalls former Topeka student Don Oden. "We pay taxes here. We are citizens here. Of course, the school board at that time felt they were giving us, you know, that old 'separate but equal' type of thing—which really turned out to be 'separate but unequal.'"

Despite inequalities, African American schools in Topeka and elsewhere were often an important resource for the African American community and a source of employment for African American professionals. Barbara Ross, a former teacher in the Topeka schools, says, "The teachers were very qualified, more so than in the white schools. Most of the black teachers had their master's

[degrees]. Other jobs were not open for our race of people." Adds historian Vanessa Siddle Walker, "Desegregation had to happen. It was imperative. It was morally right. It was constitutionally right. However, we cannot talk just about facilities and resources and the constitutional and moral reasons we had to desegregate, and discount the learning environments that were present in those schools." Another plaintiff in the Brown case, Topeka parent Vivian Scales,

says, "It wasn't that we wanted our children to go to school with white children. That was not the gist of it at all. We wanted our children to have a better and equal education, which we knew that they were not getting."

In 1896, the U.S. Supreme Court had ruled that segregation was constitutional as long as separate facilities were equal. Since the 1930s, lawyers for the National Association for the Advancement of Colored People (NAACP) had traveled throughout the South, gathering evidence to prove that segregated schools were never equal and that black schools were often desperately underfunded. By ending inequality in schools, they hoped to bring down all segregation in America.

In 1950, having laid a foundation of protests and legal challenges, the NAACP was ready to take its case to the highest court

"Why Don't You Go to School with Us?"

in the land. That year, the NAACP enlisted thirteen black parents in Topeka to serve as plaintiffs in the case they were building. They advised the parents to try to enroll their children in white schools near their homes. That fall, the Reverend Oliver Brown walked his eight-year-old daughter Linda to the Sumner School. Although brief, it would be one of the most fateful journeys of the twentieth century. Linda Brown Thompson recalls vividly, "I remember walking up the steps and how big the building seemed to me, you know, this excitement inside of me ... and I remember him going inside with the principal, and talking to him. Being young, you know, I really didn't know what was going on, but I knew something was wrong, because walking home I could feel the tension, you know, when he took me by the hand, that something was going on." Each of the Topeka children was turned away.

The case, filed as *Brown v. the Board of Education of Topeka*, went to the Supreme Court, where it was argued by Thurgood Marshall and other attorneys from the NAACP Legal Defense Fund. They spoke on behalf of plaintiffs not only in Topeka, Kansas, but also in South Carolina, Delaware, Virginia, and the District of Columbia. On May 17, 1954, Chief Justice Earl Warren announced the court's unanimous decision: "It is doubtful that any child may reasonably be expected to succeed in life if he is denied the opportunity of an education. Such an opportunity ... is a right which must be made available to all on equal terms.... Separate educational facilities are inherently unequal." Linda Brown Thompson recalls, "I was at school the day the decision

Student plaintiffs from throughout the South join in Brown v. Board of Education.

On May 17, 1954, the Supreme Court, in a unanimous decision,
strikes down the doctrine of "separate but equal" in American education.

was handed down, Mother was home. I remember her talking about this and being so excited, then when my father came in, he was overjoyed. My mother said that she remembers him embracing us and saying, 'Thanks be to God for this,' and just being overwhelmed." Plaintiff Vivian Scales also recalls her excitement: "I was at home and I was preparing supper. And the phone started ringing, you know, and I don't know whether I ever finished preparing supper or not because we were so elated, and one was calling the other one and the other one calling, the line would be busy and it was a jubilant day. It really was."

"It was a jubilant day. It really was."
—Vivian Scales,
plaintiff in
Brown v. Board
of Education

"Why Don't You Go to School with Us?"

141

In Topeka and other cities in border states, schools tended to comply with the decision. In 1954, Linda Brown was entering a junior high school that was already integrated. Her little sister would attend the newly integrated Sumner Elementary School. But integration had its costs to African Americans. Over the next two decades, more than thirty thousand African American teachers in the South would be displaced. Historian James Anderson says, "When African American teachers are kicked out of the school system, when African American principals are fired or demoted, in the name of integration, when you lose that kind of representation, from the African American vantage point we are not achieving desegregation. We may be achieving racial balance, we may be undoing the separate part of it, but we at the same time are exacerbating the unequal part of it."

Yet when the Supreme Court decision was announced in 1954, most of the South defied it. Parents and politicians vowed that white children would never sit next to black children in class. Lindsay Almond, governor of Virginia, emphatically stated, "There will be no enforced integration in Virginia." Fumed Orville Faubus, governor of Arkansas: "I will not force my people to integrate against their will. I believe in the democratic processes and principles of government wherein the people determine the problems on a local level, which is their right." Desegregation policy expert Gary Orfield explains: "The federal government versus the states was the debate, whether or not we were interfering with states' rights. And the most fervent opponents of the federal government getting into education were those people in the South who were running the apartheid school systems." In 1957, Governor Faubus of Arkansas called out the National Guard rather than allow nine black teenagers to integrate Little Rock's Central High School. His challenge was met by President Dwight Eisenhower, who sent federal troops to enforce the law. Yet integration depended on the courage of black children willing to take the first steps through the schoolhouse door. Historian James Anderson says, "Their sense was, we are going into an environment where we are not wanted. The teachers are going to be hostile. The students think of us as a despised race. We cannot make friends. We will be isolated and discriminated against. And the question for African

Black and white girls stare at each other in Fort Myer, Virginia, school following desegregation.

"Why Don't You Go to School with Us?"

143

Integrated first-grade class at the Van Buren School, Topeka, Kansas, 1957.

Americans is, do you want your children to pioneer this process? Do you want your children to pay this price?"

In other arenas, from lunch counters to voting booths, the civil rights movement was making steady gains by the early 1960s. "[It's] much easier to change the way in which we do our business," says Gary Orfield. "But when you're talking about schools, where children are socialized, people were much, much more resistant. A decade after Brown, 98 percent of black kids were still in all-black schools. Almost no white kids in the South were in black schools. There was almost no desegregation of faculty and so

forth. So the courts really failed to enforce the Brown decision and the Supreme Court didn't tighten it enough so that it really made a whole lot of difference."

Late in 1963, the nation's schoolchildren gained a new champion: a former schoolteacher, now president, named Lyndon Johnson. As a young man in Texas, Johnson had taught at a public school that served the impoverished children of Mexican American laborers. In 1966, he returned to that school. "Thirty-eight years have passed, but I still see the faces of the children who sat in my class," he said. "I still hear their eager voices speaking Span-

Student walks off school bus in Lamar, South Carolina, in front of armed National Guardsman, 1970.

"Why Don't You Go to School with Us?"

ish as I came in. I still see their excited eyes speaking friendship. I had my first lessons in the high price we pay for poverty and prejudice right here."

Johnson believed that an equal chance at education meant an equal chance at life. He created a wide-ranging series of federal programs, from Head Start to low-cost college loans, to help disadvantaged students. And he signed the Civil Rights Act of 1964, which banned discrimination on the basis of race in all federally funded programs, including schools. He then made more federal funding available, as legal expert Jay Heubert explains: "There was a carefully thought-out strategy involving a carrot and a stick. The Civil Rights Act said, among other things, that states and school districts could lose their federal funding if they refused

School: 1950–1980

*Lyndon B. Johnson
posing with other
members of the faculty
at Welhausen School,
Cotulla, Texas, 1928.*

President Lyndon B. Johnson signing the Elementary and Secondary Education Act of 1965 with his Texas grade-school teacher looking on.

to desegregate their schools. The Civil Rights Act, then, was the stick, the threat of losing federal funds. The carrot was a significant increase in federal funds that came in the form of the Elementary and Secondary Education Act of 1965."

In its first four years, the Elementary and Secondary Education Act provided an unprecedented $4 billion to aid disadvantaged students. Johnson signed the bill in Texas with his grade-school teacher looking on. "It represents a major new commitment of the federal government to quality and equality in the schooling that we offer our young people," he declared. In the South, Johnson's actions forced the issue of integration. "Most

School: 1950–1980

southern school systems [had] ignored the 1954 Brown decision," says historian Joel Spring. "But suddenly when money got involved in it, the federal government had the power then to police local school systems. They could go in and say, Are you integrated? And if you are not integrated, we're going to cut off your funds."

With this pressure from the president, new federal laws, and the civil rights movement, the South finally gave way. By 1972, 91 percent of southern black children attended integrated schools. Gary Orfield notes the enormity of this change: "In that period, in the middle 1960s and early 1970s, we took a society that was like South Africa, an apartheid society where everything was defined by race, in seventeen of our states and we made it the most integrated part of the United States. That was a huge accomplishment, an accomplishment very few democracies have ever done in peacetime. And we kind of take that for granted now, but we should never forget what we did in just a few years of serious effort."

In the 1960s, changes in the economy and technology placed growing importance on education. "To get a good job," a 1964 advertisement on television told young people, "get a good education." In affluent communities like suburban Webster Groves, Missouri, 85 percent of high school sophomores in 1966 planned to go to college. As one boy said, "My main goal is to become financially a success, and by this I mean, so I can support my family handsomely and have two cars, have a two-story house, and have sort of a high status with my friends." A female student agreed: "I think I want to be about twenty when I get married. Or else wait until I'm out of college. Because I plan to go to college. And the kind of husband I want, he has to be able to support me because I've already picked out the house that I want to live in. It's right across the street where I live now and I just love it." Yet many students didn't have such choices. "We were told by some of our teachers, 'You Mexicans are never going to amount to anything,'" remembers Severita Lara, who attended public school in Crystal City, Texas, and later became mayor. "We wanted to go to college and we wanted to take different classes [and the counselors] would tell us, 'No, you are not going to go to college.'" In the late 1960s, the struggle to equalize opportunity would also help to redefine public education in a multicultural America.

In Crystal City, Texas, 87 percent of high school students in 1968 were Mexican American, many of them the children of farmworkers. The high school principal and three out of four teachers were Anglo, as were most school board members. Whites made most decisions about student activities and the curriculum. "The textbooks did not reflect the Mexican American at all," says Lara, a student leader. "The only thing it talked about was the Mexican *bandido*, having a siesta all the time. And there was nothing positive. We couldn't see good role models about ourselves there." Another former student, Jose Angel Gutierrez, adds, "We were not allowed to speak Spanish. We would be given an option. Three days suspension, or three licks with a paddle for speaking Spanish.

"Speak English."

In the American school they wanted to make Anglos out of all of us. And they [wanted] to take our Spanish away and teach us English. Well, you don't make anybody greater by making them less." Historian Gilbert Gonzales notes, "Educational theory at the time assumed that the persistence of the Spanish language constructed a barrier to educational achievement. And so the school system assumed that this was their burden to, in a way, 'civilize' or 'Americanize' the Mexican community—and the Mexican community recoiled at that."

After graduating from Crystal City High, Jose Angel Gutierrez earned a master's degree in political science and became a leader in the Chicano civil rights movement. In 1969, he returned to Crystal City, where he helped Severita Lara and other students draw up a list of demands to the local school board. They wanted teachers to stop calling them names like "animals" and "stupid idiots," and they wanted administrators to create an educational program that respected their lives as Mexican Americans. At the Crystal City school board meeting, parents gathered in support as sixteen-year-old Severita Lara tried to present the petition. She remembers, "People were saying, yes, let's listen to them, listen to us, we want to present our demands. . . . The school board president made a motion for adjournment. And it was seconded, and they just got up and left us there. And then I turned around and told the parents, see, this is what they do to us. They don't want to listen."

The next day, five hundred students stayed out of school.

Within a week, more than two-thirds of Crystal City's high school students were on strike. "Crystal City was not unique. There were over two hundred walkouts across the nation, even in Los Angeles and other places," remembers Gutierrez. "We were trying to dramatize the unequal education that we had. Mind you, we were *for* education, which was incredible. Here you have these young kids saying, we want better education. We want more education." Students from Crystal City contacted the civil rights division of the U.S. Department of Justice, which sent federal mediators to

Students seated outside Crystal City High School, Crystal City, Texas, 1969.

"Why Don't You Go to School with Us?"

Cheerleaders from Crystal City High School, ca. 1960s. (Crystal City, Texas, is known as "The Spinach Capital of the World"; thus a Popeye statue stands on the town square.)

Students walk out, demanding equal treatment in the selection of cheerleaders at Crystal City High School, Texas, 1969.

negotiate. Severita Lara recalls, "Every demand that we made on Mexican American books, on a Mexican American class, on Mexican American teachers and a counselor was, 'If there is funds for it, we will provide it; if there is no money, we will not.' I think that was the best lesson that I ever had in politics. That that school board controlled what went on in our schools. And that being part of that school board was very important."

Having gained some concessions, students returned to school. Protesters shifted their attention to the upcoming school board

"Why Don't You Go to School with Us?"

155

Students pose in front of Crystal City High School during 1969 walkout.

election, to be held in April 1970. Through their organizing efforts, Mexican Americans gained four of seven seats on the Crystal City school board. Jose Angel Gutierrez, the twenty-six-year-old activist, became school board president. "The Monday night meetings of the school board were more powerful than the football game, and the movies on television," he recalls. "People came to the school board meetings by the hundreds to see, because every meeting was like a reform. People had been waiting for centuries for some of these changes." Crystal City's schools were transformed. Chicano history and culture were celebrated, and Spanish was spoken freely.

School: 1950–1980

In response, most white teachers and students left. But in the year after the takeover, 170 Mexican Americans who had dropped out returned to school. "We gave people pride," says Gutierrez. "We showed people that community groups can organize and take power and determine their destiny, and the destiny of their kids, that they can control the schools and the curriculum. I think also the kids themselves feel good that that they are part of the movement that made change.... It legitimized Chicano studies, with a focus on Chicanos and Mexican Americans and our contributions. And we legitimized bilingual education. It began to push from here into many, many areas and it became a national program."

Protester demands control of school board during Crystal City, Texas, walkout.

"Why Don't You Go to School with Us?"

An outgrowth of President Johnson's War on Poverty, the Bilingual Education Act offered federal money to meet the needs of children whose first language was not English. Education advisor Julian Nava says, "I was happy to be among the earliest supporters of the idea that children who could not understand the language of instruction receive instruction in the language they understood in order that they not fall behind their peers while getting special instruction in English. And then hopefully, within a year to three, a child should be able to transfer into English instruction."

In 1974, bilingual education got a boost from the U.S. Supreme Court. Lawyers had sued the San Francisco school district on behalf of eight-year-old Kenny Lau and 1800 other Chinese American elementary students. Their school held classes in English only, which few of the children understood. Jay Heubert explains: "The San Francisco schools made the argument, 'Hey, we are treating everybody here the same, what is the problem, where is the discrimination?' The Supreme Court finds that there is discrimination. Where children are different, sometimes equality of treatment requires that you treat them differently in ways that respect their educational needs."

In 1974, the federal government published teaching materials in nearly seventy languages, and allocated $68 million for bilingual programs. But the purpose of bilingual education continued to be debated. Was it to bring non-English speakers into the mainstream, as the government wanted? Or was it to preserve diverse languages and cultures, as activists in Crystal City advocated? The issue remains unresolved.

Discrimination against girls and women was another focus of school activism during this period. Less than 1 percent of all medical and law degrees awarded in 1970 went to women. "It was perfectly legal for a law school—for any institution of higher education and any professional school—to say, 'We don't need to admit women, we won't admit women,'" says Leslie Wolfe of the Center

"At Home." Gender roles portrayed in grade-school reader.

Linda and Mother Work

"Why Don't You Go to School with Us?"

for Women Policy Studies. "After Title IX was passed, that was the battering ram that opened the door."

Closely modeled after the Civil Rights Act and ratified in 1972, Title IX prohibited federal grants to schools or programs that discriminated on the basis of gender. "Passing the law was the first step; the next step was getting that law enforced," says Marcia Greenberger. "And we saw that it was going to take a lot to get the government to enforce that law."

Fourteen-year-old Dorothy Raffel was a plaintiff in a class-action suit filed in 1974 by the Women's Equity Action League. "What I was really interested in doing was playing basketball," Raffel says. "I mean I don't think I was really interested in larger issues, I wasn't interested in women's issues per se. I was really just interested in playing basketball, because that's what I enjoyed doing." As a junior high school student, Raffel spent most of her free time playing pickup basketball with older boys at the local college gym. "There wasn't any girls' after-school program," she explains. "There was nothing for the girls other than cheerleading, I believe. And so in eighth grade, I decided that I would try out for the boys' basketball team. And that wasn't viewed very receptively by the coach or anyone else. There were all kinds of wonderful comments, like if I were to try out I would have to take showers with the boys, and other sorts of enlightened comments."

"Here she was, a young girl living in State College, Pennsylvania, who had enormous skill and talent as an athlete, who wanted to play and who was simply being denied a chance to let her God-given talents come through," says attorney Marcia Greenberger. "Her school was getting federal funds. The government was responsible for giving her an opportunity and it was doing nothing." Rather than let Raffel play on the boys' team, her school created a separate program for girls. "One of the gym teachers would come and sort of stand in the gym and you could play basketball if you wanted," remembers Raffel. "So it certainly wasn't a comparable program."

Gender bias was deeply entrenched in American education, beginning with the earliest readers. "The worldview that girls and boys learned from those early textbooks was one in which girls and boys didn't do the same kinds of activities," states Leslie Wolfe. "Boys were strong, boys were masters, boys were active. Girls were sweet, girls were passive, girls watched, girls helped.... And even though you were just using that little cute book to teach a child to read, you were teaching the child what to think of the world." In upper grades, girls were often steered away from high-level courses in science and math. Boys were encouraged to excel in sports. In fact, some school districts spent up to 450 times more for boys' sports than for girls'.

Dorothy Raffel's story was one of many in the suit filed in 1974, which charged the federal government with failure to enforce Title IX. The legislation covered more than sports, but the issue of equality in school athletic programs posed one of its toughest challenges. Historian James Anderson explains, "Title IX says you can't have one basketball team and tell men and women to

"Why Don't You Go to School with Us?"

come out for it. And we simply take the best players. Title IX said yes, you should have sports for women, you should invest public resources in their development."

As the case wound its way through the courts, students and parents pressured schools to comply. Gradually, bias-free text-books and readers appeared. Vocational courses became coeducational. With more doors open to them, women began earning more than half of all undergraduate and master's degrees. And by the early 1990s, 40 percent of all high school athletes were female, up from just 1 percent in 1970. Dorothy Raffel went on to receive an athletic scholarship to college, one of the first granted to women. She eventually earned a doctorate in economics and is now a professor at Fordham University. "I'm pleased with the fact that I had the opportunity to make things easier for my daughter," Raffel says. "[So that] she won't have to sort of refight that battle." Adds Leslie Wolfe, "It's very exciting when you think that this one civil rights statute was able to generate a real movement toward equality, in not just education, not just public schools, not just K through 12, but in the professions. Because that then has an impact on the workplace."

The sweep of civil rights legislation was extended to children with disabilities, nearly 3.7 million students, in 1976. As with Title IX and bilingual education, it wasn't enough to simply treat everyone equally. Schools had to provide the resources and training to make learning possible. The changes were often costly and controversial but nonetheless widely implemented. "Efforts to achieve equality education for children with disabilities were based very heavily on Brown and the common school idea," notes legal expert Jay Heubert. "Disabled students who had been excluded said, 'Separate is inherently unequal and we deserve to be included in the same schools and classrooms as non-disabled students.' The courts accepted that argument and moreover Congress accepted that argument and enacted legislation that provided a great deal of support for the judicial decisions on the question. And in part because there is that legislative support, the rights of students with disabilities in many ways are stronger and better enforced today than the rights of any other groups."

Even as civil rights gains were made, activists in the 1970s were frustrated by an ongoing and, in places, intensifying problem. The Brown decision of 1954 had overturned segregation where it was mandated by law. But segregation was also the result of policies that governed neighborhoods and local school systems. "All northern cities were engaged in discriminatory practices," says desegregation policy expert Gary Orfield. "Historically almost all of them had been engaged in massive discrimination, both in the way they ran their schools and in the way that they ran their policies that shaped the residential pattern of their neighborhoods." Historian James Anderson notes, "Northern school boards, for instance, would zone schools, which means they would locate schools in areas to intensify segregation. At the same time there

Booker T. Washington High School, Norfolk, Virginia.

were no policies, no regulations, no laws that compelled them to do that. And so because you have this kind of institutionalized form of discrimination, it is very difficult to change it."

In 1971, the U.S. Supreme Court ruled that busing schoolchildren within city limits was a lawful remedy for segregation. Busing was used successfully to create more racially balanced schools in many cities. "Most people with children that have been bused say it was a very satisfactory experience," says Gary Orfield. "About two-thirds—blacks and whites and Latinos—all say that. ... The people that are most opposed to it are older people who have never had any direct contact with it."

But in Detroit, Michigan, busing within city limits was not seen as an effective remedy. Years of white and middle-class flight to outlying suburbs had left a citywide school-age population that was 70 percent minority and a school system—supported by an eroding tax base—in difficult straits. By contrast, just across the Detroit line, a healthier tax base supported lavish suburban schools. "You had over fifty suburban school systems surrounding Detroit," says Jay Heubert. "And in those schools there were almost all white kids. And you know, the facilities and the educational opportunities and the school funding were all much better." In 1972, a federal judge ordered a radical remedy: bus suburban students into the city and Detroit students out to the suburbs. Nearly 800,000 students would be affected.

The decision was instantly appealed in a landmark case known as *Milliken v. Bradley*. Even as it made its way to the U.S.

Black elementary pupils arrive at the Fleming School on Detroit's East Side,
Monday morning, January 26, 1976, as court-ordered busing begins.

Supreme Court, the political climate was shifting. Busing aroused growing controversy and became a popular target for politicians, including President Richard Nixon. "We have found that where we have heavy reliance on cross-city busing of schoolchildren, it has failed to meet either of its intended purposes," he said. "It has failed to promote quality education for all, and it's failed to end the racial isolation which we all agree must be ended." In 1974, a conservative Supreme Court reversed the Detroit decision, finding that the suburbs bore no responsibility for conditions in urban schools. Any plan to desegregate would be limited to the city itself. Two decades after Brown, Thurgood Marshall, now a Supreme Court Justice, sharply dissented in the Detroit decision: "In the short run, it may seem the easier course to allow our great metropolitan areas to be divided up into two cities—one white, the other black. But it is a course, I predict, our people will ultimately regret. For unless our children begin to learn together, there is little hope that our people will ever learn to live together."

According to Jay Heubert, the Supreme Court's decision "sent a message to parents that if they could simply leave the urban district and make it across the district lines into the suburbs, they would not be part of any kind of desegregation plan involving the suburbs. The long-term consequences of this in my view have been catastrophic. They have increased significantly the concentrations of minority people and especially poor people in our urban centers even as our suburban districts become wealthier and whiter in many places." Gary Orfield believes that school desegre-

gation will have to be pursued nationwide despite the recent re-
treat from the policy. "The census bureau projects that the
majority of school-age children in the United States will be non-
white by about 2030," he says. "The majority of all people in the
country will be [non-white] by about 2050. It's not going to be an
option about whether or not we mess up the incorporation of one-
tenth or one-eighth of our population into the mainstream; we are
talking about a situation where whites will be one of a number of
different minorities in a society where there isn't any majority.
And we have to live together and figure out how to make that
work. How we do that without living together in neighborhoods or
going to school together is a mystery to me."

In 1980, the campaign for equality in America's schools was not
yet complete. Yet in just thirty years, radical change had occurred, in part due to the intervention of the courts and the federal government. Educators then as now would argue the consequences. Historian David Tyack says, "We have had many
debates about affirmative action, about desegregation, about
what is feminism anyway, about are special needs children getting
too much money—but I would argue that to have debates and action is precisely where we should be in a democratic society, instead of sweeping disadvantages under the rug and social injustice
under the rug. We sometimes forget where we were in 1954 and
I see a net gain for the society." Chester Finn, assistant secretary
at the Department of Education under Reagan, states, "I don't
doubt that some things are better off and I think that not being

Supreme Court Justice Thurgood Marshall.

able to discriminate against kids on the basis of their skin color is progress for the society—but it sure led to a lot of litigation and lawsuits and busing programs and white-flight activities and a whole slew of other things that many people would regard as having been harmful to the quality and performance of education and the health of the democracy." These issues, along with the introduction of new, free-market strategies, would help drive the reforms of the next two decades.

Part Four

1980-2000

THE

BOTTOM

LINE

Introduction

LARRY CUBAN

*There is hardly any work we can do or any expenditures we can make
that will yield so large a return to our industries as would come from the
establishment of educational institutions which would give us skilled hands
and trained minds for the conduct of our industries and our commerce.*

THEODORE SEARCH
President of the National Association
of Manufacturers, 1898[1]

*Education isn't just a social concern, it's a major economic issue. If our students
can't compete today, how will our companies compete tomorrow? In an age
when a knowledgeable work force is a nation's most important resource, American
students rank last internationally in calculus and next to last in algebra.*

JOHN AKERS
Chairman of IBM, 1991[2]

1. Cited in Herbert Kliebard, *Schooled to Work: Vocationalism and the American Curriculum, 1876–1946.*
2. Ad appearing in the *New York Times Magazine*, April 28, 1991, p. 21.

At two separate points in our history, the ends of the nineteenth and twentieth centuries, American schools have been vocationalized. Among the civic, academic, and moral goals that have historically guided tax-supported public schools, one became primary: preparing students for the ever-changing workplace. Twice in the past, business-led coalitions forged political alliances among public officials, union leaders, educators, and parents. Fearing foreign competition for their share of the global market, they turned to schools to develop an efficient workforce that would give American international trade an edge and ultimately fuel prosperity. In both cases, these reformers believed that schools should be modeled after the corporation and the marketplace. In these two periods of reform, business involvement in U.S. public schools was sustained and influential in changing school goals, governance, management, organization, and curriculum. But, surprisingly, business support has done little to alter dominant classroom practices.

For corporate leaders so committed to enhancing their firms' profits, the "bottom line," classroom teaching and learning has become their educational bottom line. But it is precisely here that the impact of business-led coalitions has had little influence. How can that be?

Business interest in schools has largely involved private individuals and groups drawn from a variety of large, middle-sized, and small businesses. No monolithic business community, "Big Business," has shaped and steered U.S. public schools. Of course, corporate elites have existed (and continue to exist) in the United States. And, yes, private businesses are highly organized and possess political resources that many other interest groups lack. But the diversity of business involvement (multinational Fortune 500 companies, regional and national business associations, and local chambers of commerce) in a wide range of school reform activities has been far more typical than any narrowly based group of individual corporate leaders who have sought single-mindedly to change U.S. schools in the past or now.

Since the founding of tax-supported public schools in the mid-nineteenth century, educators, public officials, and a broad band of business leaders (but by no means all) have worked together to improve schooling. These political alliances saw schools as economically important in producing a literate workforce that could help companies compete in the marketplace. They believed

School: 1980–2000

that more and better schooling would not only build citizens but also bolster the economy.

Over the past century, businesses have started schools, helped educators manage, donated cash and equipment, persuaded children and teachers of the importance of a market economy, and subsidized programs aimed at enhancing teacher knowledge and skills. In the policy arena, business leaders formed coalitions of like-minded executives to lobby state and federal legislators to enact particular education bills.

In the 1880s and 1890s, top industrialists expressed strong fears that U.S. products were losing ground to those made in Britain and Germany. When American business leaders traveled to Germany to determine how the country had so quickly become a world trade rival to Great Britain, they often pointed to the fact that German technical schools were graduating highly skilled workers.

In the years prior to World War I, an alliance evolved among American business leaders, top public officials, unions, and progressive educators who were highly critical of traditional schooling. Teachers talked most of the time; children listened, read the textbooks, and recited answers to their teachers. By contrast, progressive educators wanted teachers to involve students in planning what to study and to have students learn by working on real-life projects. Other reformers sought to copy the successes of German technical education. By 1910, different reformers came together in the vocational education movement. Yet progressive classroom reforms became subordinate to the larger goal of preparing workers for an industrial economy that could secure a larger share of global markets.

Fears of foreign economic competition and the belief that vocationally driven American schools could strengthen the domestic economy led business leaders to privately fund vocational schools and then coax school boards to take over their funding and operation. In 1917, the vocational education coalition for the first time succeeded in securing federal subsidies for industrial courses in American schools. But this introduction of vocational education into U.S. schools was far from the only influence that this business-led alliance had on schooling.

Many political and educational reformers, even while condemning business-

The Bottom Line

men as robber barons, admired their insistence on scientific efficiency and professional management. A new breed of reform-minded educators, attracted to the higher social status that corporate leaders had attained, saw strong parallels between running a business and a school system.

These school reformers borrowed heavily from the values, language, organization, and governance of corporate leaders and applied them to schools. "Administrative progressives," as these reformers have been called, detested the large, politically appointed school boards of fifty to one hundred members who put friends and relatives into teaching and principal positions and took company bribes to buy their textbooks. They wanted nonpartisan elections and smaller, appointed school boards that prized efficiency and professionally trained managers. They sought nonpolitical boards of directors just like those running corporations. By 1930, this wing of progressive reformers had converted most school boards into smaller, businesslike operations with modern managerial practices divorced from partisan politics.

Thus, between 1880 and 1930 major domestic economic changes and U.S. expansion into world markets had much influence on public schooling. Corporate leaders and business associations viewed schools as crucial in producing a trained workforce that would strengthen American international competitiveness. They started private vocational schools and secured federal funding for vocational courses in secondary schools. By 1930, most urban secondary schools had vocational guidance counselors and a separate vocational track; many cities had separate vocational high schools. Instruction in these classes differed distinctly from that of academic courses. Teachers had students actively involved in designing, making, repairing, and completing real-life work projects that had apparent cash value outside of school.

Moreover, school reformers had adopted the corporate model of efficient school governance. They moved from large, politically appointed school boards and untrained administrators to small, elected boards filled with business and civic-minded laypersons who hired professionally trained experts to run their schools. This pattern continued into the late twentieth century when the second major instance of business involvement in schools occurred.

Beginning in the mid-1970s, the decline of U.S. workplace productivity, rising unemployment, losses in market share to Japan and Germany, and swift changes in technologies led corporate leaders and public officials to try to determine reasons for the poor performance of the American economy. Within a few years, a crescendo of criticism over high school graduates unprepared for the workplace, poor scores on national tests, violence in urban schools, and the flight of white middle-class families from cities to suburbs fixed blame on American public schools. Corporate and public officials organized political action groups called Business Roundtables to attack the problem of inefficient and ineffective schools.

By 1983, a presidential commission of corporate and public leaders and educators had reported their assessment of public schools in "A Nation At Risk." This report crystallized the growing sense of unease with public schooling in the business community by tightly coupling mediocre student performance on national and international tests to mediocre economic performance in the global marketplace.

Following publication of "A Nation At Risk," state after state increased high school graduation requirements, lengthened the school year, and added more tests. In 1989, in an unprecedented act President George Bush convened the fifty governors to discuss education. They called for six national goals (later expanded to eight), one of which asked American students to rank first on international tests in math and science by the year 2000. Throughout the 1990s, states mandated curricular and performance standards, new tests, and accountability of principals, teachers, and students for test scores. Instead of seeking high school graduates with industrial and craft skills that an earlier generation of business-led reformers wanted, the agenda now called for tougher academic courses and higher test scores on national and international tests for all students, not just those going on to college.

Three key assumptions drove this alliance of public officials, corporate leaders, and educators. The first held that in the same way the economy becomes more efficient and prosperous when businesses compete freely in the marketplace and consumers make choices among varied products, public schools would become more efficient and effective if they competed with one another and gave parents choices of where to send their children. The second maintained that in an information-based economy, students will perform better in the workplace if they have taken rigorous academic subjects, especially math

The Bottom Line

and science. The final assumption was that although schools, unlike businesses, show no profits and losses—no bottom line—at the end of the year, standardized test scores measure what has been learned and can roughly predict how future employees will perform in the workplace.

Given these assumptions, reformers designed solutions that essentially copied business practices. The corporate formula for success was crisp: set clear goals and high standards for employees. Restructure operations so that managers and employees who actually make the product decide how it is to be done efficiently and effectively. Then hold those managers and employees responsible for the quality of the product by rewarding those who meet or exceed their goals and punishing those who fail.

Top corporate leaders and Business Roundtables claimed that these strategies had worked for Ford Motor Company, IBM, Xerox, Hewlett-Packard, and scores of other firms. If schools pursued these changes, they could revolutionize public schooling.

How does this corporate model of success fit nearly fifteen thousand school boards where lay citizens—not experts—make policy in public sessions, tell professionals what they must do, and declare no dividend to stockholders at the end of the fiscal quarter? Despite the substantial differences between public school governance and businesses, a number of measures recommended by business alliances are now common in schools today: establish clear national goals and high academic standards; give parents choices among schools; let schools compete for students; test students often; tell parents and taxpayers exactly how their children and schools are doing on these tests by issuing periodic report cards; recognize and reward those staff members, students, and schools that meet goals; shame and punish those that fail to meet the standards; and reduce costs by contracting out certain tasks to private firms.

Borrowing heavily from the private sector, this formula for public school improvement crossed political party lines. Since the early 1980s, both Republican and Democratic presidents have endorsed this strategy and directed federal education officials to support it. State governors and legislatures have moved swiftly to establish curricular standards, measure performance through standardized tests, and hold teachers and administrators responsible for student

School: 1980–2000

outcomes on these tests with such devices as cash payments and takeovers of failing schools and districts.

Parents' choices in selecting their children's schools have also expanded dramatically in recent years. Private companies now run public schools. More than two thousand independent charter schools exist. A few state-designed experiments give vouchers or checks to parents for use in private schools. In short, the corporate model of market competition, choice, and accountability has been largely copied by districts and states and has spread swiftly.

The wholesale application of a business model for success is only part of the private-sector influence on public schools. Other administrative influences are apparent as well. Managerial strategies derived from business include contracting school functions to private firms and importing "Total Quality Management" from the private sector. Schools now use technology for improved communication, resource management, and to aid teaching and learning. The rapid spread of computers in public schools in less than two decades has reduced the national number of students per computer from over 125 in the early 1980s to about 9 in 1998. Commercialization of curriculum and instruction has expanded. Channel One television, which is now in one-quarter of all high schools, displays ads in exchange for supplying free equipment; schools receive funds for signing exclusive contracts on selling soft drinks and for selling advertising space.

Missing from this inventory of business influences is teaching and learning. Have business approaches altered what routinely occurs in classrooms between teachers and students? Apart from the commercialization of some instructional materials, Channel One television, and other business influences, it is difficult to determine whether teachers now teach differently than they did before the early 1980s, when private-sector involvement in America's public schools began to build.

The few studies that have been done about teaching and learning in actual classrooms before the 1980s and since confirm that dominant patterns of teacher-centered instruction in both elementary and secondary schools have remained stable. If anything, the impact of standards-based performance and accountability for test score improvement has hardened these traditional

The Bottom Line

teaching practices. Once-flourishing progressive classroom approaches such as portfolios, project-based teaching, and performance-based testing that blossomed between the mid-1980s and early 1990s, for example, have since shriveled under the unrelenting pressure for higher test scores.

As a consequence of almost two decades of business involvement through philanthropy, partnerships, and imitation of corporate practices, public schools have become more businesslike in governance, management, and organization. As school districts have come to prize business savvy, big-city school boards have abandoned educators and chosen from the ranks of former CEOs, top military officers, and high government officials. More competition exists among public schools. Parents have far more choices among schools than they did a quarter-century ago.

Moreover, in the last twenty years, the political alliance of business leaders, public officials, and educators has succeeded in standardizing the academic curriculum and requiring it of all students. Vocational courses aimed at equipping students to move directly into the workplace have largely withered away, replaced by a trend toward vocationalizing all academic subjects—that is, every student must take so many years of English, social studies, math, and science to prepare for the workplace. The one exception to all of these changes is in classroom teaching itself; if anything, reformers have ended up strengthening traditional instructional practices while weakening progressive ones.

Kindergartens have become increasingly more academic to prepare children for the first grade; middle schools have become increasingly more like high schools; and vocational education courses have steadily declined as high schools have become increasingly college preparatory. Ensuring that American schools produce fully prepared graduates who can perform well in the workplace has led to an intense concentration on achieving high test scores in academic skills and subjects and a hardening of already dominant patterns of teacher-centered instruction. In effect, a single model of good teaching and good schools has emerged as a political orthodoxy from this concentration on harnessing public schools to the economy.

Finally, the ironies of corporate influence have become visible. A century ago, popular support for major reforms in school governance, organization, curriculum, and instruction made business leaders into administrative and

School: 1980–2000

pedagogical progressives. In those decades, corporate leaders promoted more vocational courses and fewer academic courses, more hands-on learning than reading from books, and more real-life experiences rather than listening to teachers. That political coalition succeeded in adding vocational education to the curriculum. Although learning-by-doing classroom practices were limited, business leaders maintained that there was more than one version of good teaching and good schools.

Now, a century later, the coalition of business leaders, public officials, and educators say that more and tougher academic subjects equip graduates with essential knowledge and skills not only to perform well in an information-based workplace but also to secure America's global economic supremacy. Reformers called for and got a uniform academic curriculum that all students take at the price of eliminating vocational subjects. Reformers demanded and received more tests; now teachers, using traditional methods of teaching, spend more time with students preparing for tests, and students who fail these tests are left back for another year or don't graduate. Some teachers who were following progressive practices in their classrooms continue to use them, but many have forsaken their beliefs, and others have adopted practices they find distasteful.

What business-minded reformers sought in the school curriculum, tests, and accountability has largely been achieved in current state and local policies and programs at the cost of freezing the very teaching practices that an earlier generation of business-led reformers severely criticized.

So I return to where I began. Fear of foreign competition and fiercely held beliefs that education harnessed to the economy will strengthen the nation's global competitive position prompted sustained and influential political involvement by a variety of business leaders twice in the past century. Although business-led alliances have been limited in what they could achieve, particularly in shaping what occurs in classrooms, many documented changes in public schooling can be attributed to the involvement of corporate leaders, especially the hammering of alternative versions of good teaching and good schools into one mold for all students.

And what do these changes amount to? Given the sparse evidence, very little. No one can say for sure whether increased choice and competition have improved students' academic performance. The scanty evidence available on

The Bottom Line

whether standardized test scores are connected to job performance suggests that they are not linked. The idea that businesses need high school graduates who have taken more math and science to perform effectively in work has not been studied much, and what evidence exists raises serious doubts about this popular connection. Finally, where the bottom line matters in schooling—the classroom—no one knows for certain whether all the testing, all the required courses, and all the penalties and rewards get teachers to teach better and students to learn more.

Even more damning are questions omitted from current political agendas for school reform. In what ways does turning schooling into a consumer product, no different from candy bars and cars, undermine the common good that tax-supported public schools historically served? Do schools geared to preparing workers also build literate, active, and morally sensitive citizens who carry out their civic duties? How can schools develop independently thinking citizens who earn their living in corporate workplaces? What happens when the economy hiccups, unemployment increases, and graduates have little money to secure higher education or find a job matched to their skills? Will public schools, now an arm of the economy, get blamed—as they have in the past—for creating the mismatch? These basic questions, unasked by business-inspired reform coalitions over the past century, go unanswered today.

A Nation at Risk?

You can't teach a child how to think unless
you have something for him to think about.

GEORGANN REAVES

Indiana student takes statewide assessment exam, 1988.

By the 1980s, education in the United States had reached unprecedented levels. Almost the entire school-age population was enrolled. More than 71 percent of seventeen-year-olds graduated from high school, and the majority continued on to college. But to some, including President Ronald Reagan, these numbers masked widespread problems. "Our educational system is in the grips of a crisis caused by low standards, lack of purpose, and a failure to strive for excellence," Reagan said in 1983, as he launched a campaign for reform. "Our agenda is to restore quality to education by increasing competition and by strengthening parental choice and local control."

A "learning crisis" is declared by politicians and the press in the mid-1970s and early 1980s.

Reports of a "learning crisis" by politicians and the press would forever change the way Americans perceived their schools. And they would open the door to free-market reforms that challenged basic ideals of public education, while introducing concepts such as consumer choice and economic competition. Traditionally, America's public schools had aimed to educate citizens to live in a democracy. They were the melting pot in which immigrants embraced the American dream. And they were at the forefront of the struggle for equality. In the 1980s and 1990s, schools were also asked to compete in a business-driven world where one thing mattered: the bottom line.

December 8, 1975 / 75 cents

Newsweek

Why Johnny Can't Write

School: 1980–2000

The twentieth century's final wave of school reform began with a 1983 report to President Reagan titled "A Nation At Risk." Commissioned by the U.S. Department of Education, the report said that the poor quality of America's schools posed a threat to the welfare of the country. Historian David Tyack summarizes: "It said, 'Look, we are going to hell in a handbasket. If some foreign power had done to us educationally what we have done to ourselves'—said the report—'then we would consider it an act of war.' " The language "built up and up and up," Tyack adds. "And that fit the mood of the Reagan years.... It was a text for the times."

The statistics compiled for the report seemed to indicate a shocking drop in test scores and student achievement. More than 40 percent of students, "A Nation At Risk" said, were unprepared either for work or for college. Yet many educators cried foul, citing other evidence that showed more students doing better academi-

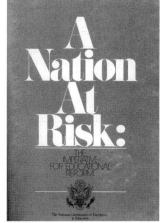

A Nation at Risk?

cally than ever before. As author Nicholas Lemann notes, "The best source of data to counteract 'A Nation At Risk' is probably NAEP—the National Assessment of Education Progress—which goes back for at least a couple of decades before that and just doesn't show this dire picture of steady decline. It shows things, you know, slowly rising." Historian Carl Kaestle agrees. "Not only is it not true that there has been a great decline since that time," he says, "but it is also true that we are educating a much wider proportion of our population now than we were in the 1950s."

In addition, many educators disagreed with comments made by Reagan in 1983, in which he suggested that civil rights enforcement had hurt basic education over the previous two decades. "The schools were charged by the federal courts with leading in the correcting of long-standing injustices in our society," Reagan said. "Racial segregation. Sex discrimination. Lack of opportunity for the handicapped. Perhaps there was just too much to do in too little time." In fact, says historian James Anderson, "groups that had lagged way behind and had not had access to good public education were making significant strides during the same time period. And so in some ways, our schools were doing a better job in important areas than they had ever done historically, and yet all of that was lost because of our concern over the economy, which we blamed on the schools."

The U.S. economy faced new threats from global competitors. The auto industry, for example, had been losing ground to Japanese manufacturers since the 1970s. As had happened in the 1950s

after the Soviets beat the Americans into space, blame was placed on American schooling. The authors of "A Nation At Risk" claimed that economic security depended on education reform. They recommended higher standards for graduation, more courses in traditional subjects and in the new field of "computer science," a longer school day and school year, and more home-work. At the same time, the federal government was scaling back its role in education and shifting the burden of these reforms to state and local authorities. They, in turn, cracked down on students. And to ensure that students were meeting these new standards, an era of high-stakes testing was born.

While many debated the dire conclusions of "A Nation At Risk," few argued that reform was needed in some schools. This was especially true in the nation's cities, where per-pupil spending might be as low as a third of what it was in nearby suburbs. But without additional funding, how could these schools improve? Some reformers believed that one solution was to apply business strategies, such as consumer choice and economic competition. "You want to improve public education?" says John Golle, founder and chairman of Education Alternatives, Inc., a for-profit company. "The way to do it is compete with them. Allow them the chance to compete with private enterprise, and vice versa. That's the way you're going to make public education better."

Injecting competition into America's urban school systems was the strategy behind an experiment already under way in East Har-lem, a school district of 14,000 mostly low-income students in New

A Nation at Risk?

York City. In the mid-1970s, East Harlem ranked last among New York's thirty-two school districts. "It was consistently thirty-second," notes Seymour Fliegel, a school administrator in East Harlem at the time. "It didn't move to thirty-one or thirty. So there was a tremendous advantage to being at the bottom. You can afford to be a risk taker."

In 1974, educators in East Harlem asked some of the district's best teachers to create small, alternative public schools, carving space as needed within existing buildings. "My first reaction was, 'You must be kidding,' " says Deborah Meier, founder and former principal of East Harlem's Central Park East Schools. "I had never heard of anybody offering to do that in the public system. And it was the beginning of a very bold and exciting experiment.

Within ten years, East Harlem went from having twenty schools to having fifty-two schools in the same buildings." Each school had its own focus and style, notes Fliegel. "So you had the open ed, progressive schools. We had some highly traditional schools; at the Frederick Douglass Academy they [wore] uniforms. We had three math and science schools. We had a maritime school, we had a sports school, we had a writing school, two performing-arts schools. Keep in mind, though, the goals were always the same: raising academic achievement. The themes were different ways to motivate the youngsters to get there."

By 1982, educators in East Harlem required that all junior high students choose a school, whether alternative or regular; no schools would be assigned. Any school that was failing would be

Students at Central Park East Secondary High School in East Harlem, New York.

A Nation at Risk?

shut down and reorganized, much like a failing business. "Well, what do you think happened in the regular schools?" asks Seymour Fliegel. "Do you think they said, 'Look, isn't that nice, in the alternative schools their kids are doing well. They get into good schools. And we just sit here'? They started developing better schools. So in East Harlem, some of the regular schools were better than the alternative schools in their buildings. I was very happy about that."

By 1987, East Harlem was outperforming half of the city's school districts. Many attributed the turnaround to the smaller, more personalized schools. Most agreed that choice had also played a critical role. Deborah Meier states, "I think choice offers us the opportunity to rethink what we mean by a public institution and stop thinking of public institutions as dull, boring, mediocre buildings that house bureaucrats. Instead think of them as lively, coherent places that represent the very best and most excellent standards."

In 1992, New York began allowing students to seek enrollment in any public school in the city. Yet there were so few alternative schools, and so few students willing or able to leave their regular schools, that little competition resulted. Nationwide, a small but growing number of parents went to great lengths to get their children enrolled in a small number of specialized and alternative public schools. These included magnet schools, designed to combat segregation by attracting high-caliber students of diverse backgrounds. Magnet schools often received extra funding in

School choice rally in Cleveland, Ohio, June 20, 2000.

order to offer high-quality programs in the arts, science, and mathematics.

The interest in finding alternatives to local public schools, rather than working to improve those schools, has raised some concern. Historian Carl Kaestle comments, "I think that what is dominating the argument about choice is a very privatistic kind of mentality. Not that the schools will be private, but that the motives for going to school are more private. Getting your kid ahead ... making your kid's scores come out higher." Jonathan Kozol, an advocate for children in low-income communities, adds, "There is a tendency in many cities nowadays to develop a kind of lifeboat mentality where the politicians and some of the educators sort of sigh and say, well, we are not going to save most of these kids, let's at least start a number of very attractive, spectacular little schools. The trouble is, these types of schools tell us nothing about what's happening to the majority of children in that city."

One of the most controversial forms of public school choice is a program known as vouchers, which allows students to use public school funds to pay for private schools. Voucher supporters believe that competition from private schools will force public schools to improve. "It's just like anything else—a supermarket, a car dealership," says Annette Polly Williams, State Assemblywoman from Wisconsin. "You keep selling lemons, then you're going to wonder why nobody's coming to buy your cars. What you have to do is get you some good cars and people will come and buy it. So public school around this nation is selling something that nobody wants."

School: 1980–2000

At Williams's urging, and despite widespread opposition, Wisconsin passed the country's first voucher legislation. In 1990, the year it was implemented, a group of nearly four hundred low-income students in Milwaukee attended private, nonreligious schools at taxpayer expense. The private schools got $2,500 from the state for each student, money that would have otherwise gone to public school funding. Critics feared that an expansion of the voucher program might ultimately cripple the city's public schools. Voucher proponent Annette Polly Williams defended the program. "I am not in this battle on education to save any institution," she said. "I am in here to save the lives of children by any means necessary."

Nationwide, voucher advocates got a boost in 1992 from President George Bush. "For too long, we've shielded schools from competition, allowed our schools a damaging monopoly power over our children," Bush said. "It is time we began thinking of a system of public education in which many providers offer a marketplace of opportunities. . . . A revolution is under way in Milwaukee and across this country, a revolution to make American schools the best in the world." Chester Finn, an education advisor to Reagan, adds, "Well, the best argument for choice is to enable poor people to have the same rights and opportunities that rich people already have by virtue of being rich. I mean, rich people exercise school choice. They move to where they want to buy a house, because of the schools, or they send their kid to a private school. It is poor people who typically get trapped in bad schools and can't afford to

A Nation at Risk?

do anything about it." Jonathan Kozol counters, "They are proposing a voucher of a couple thousand dollars which at best would allow a handful of poor children or children of color to go to a pedagogically marginal private school. The day that the conservative voucher advocates in America tell me that they would like to give every inner-city black, Hispanic, or poor white kid a $25,000 voucher to go to Exeter, I will become a Republican."

By 1997, the Milwaukee voucher program served 1,500 students. Success stories included Urban Day, an elementary school offering small classes and a rigorous curriculum, whose students went on to graduate from high school at double the norm for the area. But many private schools did not accept vouchers, and the quality of those that did varied widely. "Anybody can start a choice school in Milwaukee," says Greg Doyle of the Wisconsin Department of Public Instruction. "You don't have to have any money. You don't have to have any expertise in education. We had quite a number of people who wanted to start school without a building, without teachers, without textbooks. We believe that those are conditions that are not conducive to the education of children in the state." Critics also noted that the private schools, unlike public schools, could cater to special interests. The Bruce Guadeloupe School, for example, stressed Hispanic heritage and achievement. The Harambee School, visited by Vice President Dan Quayle in 1994, was Afrocentric.

Of greater concern to voucher opponents, however, was the push to include private religious schools. In 1994, this expansion

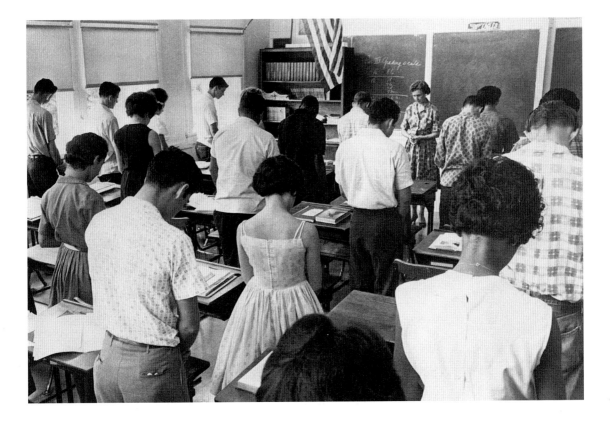

was debated in the Wisconsin legislature. Annette Polly Williams, a voucher proponent, told members, "I am not convinced that God or religion is going to hurt these little children in these schools." Opponents went to court, arguing that the use of publicly funded vouchers in religious schools violated the constitutional separation of church and state. "The question is, if it is okay for one church, why is it not okay for another church?" says Greg Doyle. "Would the taxpayer generally be willing to support a voucher that went to a school run by witches? Would they be willing to support a school that was run by skinheads? The gravest

Students praying at the start of the school day in San Antonio, Texas, in 1962.

A Nation at Risk?

195

concern has to be that this society made a decision in its very beginning that church and state would be separate. And so we believe that the democracy needs that separation." Chester Finn argues, "I don't get this distinction between why it is okay to assist people in church-affiliated hospitals and church-affiliated colleges and church-affiliated day care centers—but for some reason it is verboten to assist them in a church-affiliated elementary or secondary school." Jonathan Kozol says, "Think of cities that are just struggling to hold together . . . and then imagine what it would be like if you added a system whereby every little intellectual, ethnic, theological splinter group could indoctrinate children separately, and use public money to do it. It would rip apart the social fabric of this nation."

In 1996, low-income students in Cleveland, Ohio, became the first in the nation to use vouchers to attend religious schools. Two years later, in 1998, the Wisconsin Supreme Court allowed Milwaukee students to do the same. That fall, the number of voucher students jumped to nearly six thousand. Significantly, three out of four of these students had already been enrolled in private schools but now paid for them with public school money. This left the majority of Milwaukee's public schools with fewer resources than before. "One of our biggest concerns about the choice program is that we are not making the effort to improve the public schools," says Greg Doyle. "Rather than supporting the public schools we are supplanting them with something else. An expanded voucher system is going to require the taxpayer to support more than just

School: 1980–2000

Milwaukee voucher students attending religious schools.

Milwaukee voucher students attending religious schools.

the public schools in America. It is going to require them to support an entire private school system. In Wisconsin, that will mean about six hundred and sixty million additional dollars for education in this state and we don't have the money for that."

To critics nationwide, voucher programs threaten public schools not only by siphoning off resources, but also by selectively sorting through students and excluding those who are difficult or harder to serve. Says James Anderson, "We could end up with vouchers that would allow systems to cater to people on the basis of class. People who are well-to-do [could] select students who are very similar in terms of class background and educate them in a

School: 1980–2000

very different system. And we might end up, particularly in large metropolitan areas, with another class of schools that are public schools for the poor, the disenfranchised."

Still another movement for school choice gained momentum during this period: home schooling. By the late 1990s, the Christian right had led a successful campaign to make home schooling legal in all fifty states. While the percentage of students being home schooled remained small—less than 2.5 percent in 2000—exit strategies like vouchers and home schooling would continue to spark political battles in the years ahead.

Baltimore, Maryland, was the site of another experiment with

A child demonstrates in favor of home schooling at the State Capitol in Harrisburg, Pennsylvania, 1985.

A Nation at Risk?

big implications: private management of public schools. Schools in Baltimore were in tough shape in 1992, when the experiment began. "We were overcrowded, underfunded," says Irene Dandridge, president of the Baltimore Teachers Union from 1980 to 1996. "Lots of teachers did not have supplies, such things as paper and duplicating fluid." Teachers had to buy their own books and buy workbooks for children, she says. "Having to duplicate materials over and over and then not having the paper to do it with. It was bad, it really was." Dr. Walter Amprey, Baltimore superintendent of schools from 1991 to 1997, adds, "We had tried many things in the past. I had a real clear list of what wasn't working. Not a real strong list of what would work. So I was looking for answers where they hadn't been found before."

John T. Golle, head of Education Alternatives, Inc., the first for-profit company to manage an American public school, talks with first- and second-graders at Tesseract School in Eagan, Minnesota, in 1995.

School: 1980–2000

In 1992, the city of Baltimore hired a private company, Education Alternatives Inc., or EAI, to manage nine of its public schools. "[Public schools] are funded by the government. Their rules and regulations are dictated by the government," says John Golle, founder and chairman of EAI. "Where else can we look in our society and say that a government monopoly functions best for our society? I would suggest to you, no place."

For the same $5,400 per pupil that the city would have spent, EAI said that it could run the schools, boost test scores, and still make a profit. A Minnesota-based company, EAI was already running two private schools, as well as a public school near Miami, Florida—the first in the nation to be managed by a private business. Yet private-sector involvement in education is not new, says Jeanne Allen, president of the Center for Education Reform. "We buy our desks, they are for profit, we buy our pencils, we buy our computers. We get our software, teachers are paid. I mean, there is money all around our schools. So to have a private company come in is not really a strange idea." In Baltimore, John Golle focused on the school buildings, which were in a state of disrepair. As a private company, EAI could bypass the bureaucracy, invest its own money, and hire outside contractors to rehab the buildings. He remembers, "When people came in and they saw one high-speed computer for every four kids, they said, how did you do this and earn a profit? We said it is easy. We had everyone compete. Compete for the delivery of the food services. Compete for the maintenance and the cleaning of the building, interior and exterior. And

A Nation at Risk?

by competing what we found was we were able to drive up the quality and drive down the costs."

Critics held a different view. EAI had replaced unionized teacher's aides with interns paid an hourly wage. They had cut special education services in half, and reduced art and music programs. The company was accused of taking profits back to Minnesota at the expense of Baltimore's schoolchildren. "These children need many, many, more services than children that you might find in the suburbs, for example, than most children," Irene Dandridge argues. "They need psychological services, the city has to provide health services. All kinds of services that children just cannot learn without. There is just not enough money in public school education, particularly in urban centers, to have a profit and good education, too."

Elsewhere, corporate involvement in schools was growing. By the mid-1990s, education in the United States was a $300-billion-a-year industry. Increasingly, for-profit tutoring firms were brought into classrooms to raise student test scores. School districts earned extra cash by allowing corporate logos to appear in public school buildings. Whittle Communications offered free media equipment to schools. In exchange, all students had to watch twelve minutes per day of Channel One, a broadcast of news features and commercials geared to a young audience. By the year 2000, one-quarter of the nation's secondary students were watching Channel One.

The controversial partnership between corporations and

schools brought national attention to the EAI experiment in Baltimore. Stockholders had seen the price of their shares rise from $4 to $49 in the first two years. But for students, the gains were less clear. An independent report said that EAI students performed no better on tests than their peers in other Baltimore schools. "There are other parts of our school system that did better for our school system than EAI," Kurt Schmoke, the mayor of Baltimore at that time, said. City leaders, caught in a fiscal crisis, pressured the board of education to end the experiment early. In 1995, with one swift vote, the school privatization experiment in Baltimore ended, just three years after it began. In news coverage of the cancellation, Bob Kur of NBC News said, "Had it gone better in Baltimore, this movement to privatize schools could have spread all over the country. This was a crucial test for one of the most controversial experiments in American public education."

Those involved disagreed over what had been learned. Union leader Irene Dandridge: "Their primary job was supposed to be education. And the education part just didn't work. Cleaning the buildings worked. Bringing in supplies worked. Teachers were happy to get them, certainly. But they did not deliver the quality of education that they promised." Superintendent Walter Amprey: "It started the concept of schools making their own decisions about their dollars—and beginning to contract on their own. And we did put in place, through the EAI relationship, a way in which schools could begin to spend their own dollars as opposed to having those dollars spent for them by the central office." EAI

A Nation at Risk?

chairman John Golle: "This is going to be the example that people refer back to and say, 'Private enterprise can't work internally to make the system better; they are not welcome. Private enterprise will have to work externally to make competition prevail and make the whole system better.' In the last two years, there have been a dozen or more companies coming to the forefront, running charter schools all over the nation and proving that very point."

One way that EAI has found to work externally is through a special category of public schools known as charter schools. "Charter schools are a new form of public school," explains Jeanne Allen. "[They are] the same as traditional public schools in that they are open to everyone. They are not private, they don't have admissions criteria. They don't cost money. And oftentimes they are run by teachers, and parents are heavily involved." Charter schools can also be run by private companies; in 1997, EAI signed a contract with the state of Arizona to run a dozen small charter schools. Proponents argue that charter schools offer more flexibility than other public schools, in part because most are accountable directly to the state, rather than to city or school bureaucracies. Seymour Fliegel, who helped to pioneer school choice in East Harlem and is now a leading advocate of school choice, explains, "There is no central board, there is no district office, there is no superintendent, you make a contract that is usually five years, three to five years, you say this is where youngsters will be achievement-wise. If you reach those goals, you get renewed. If you don't, they can close you down."

School: 1980–2000

As schools that must be chosen, rather than assigned, charters compete for students with targeted programs in subjects such as environmental science, learning and manners, and performing arts. Supporters hope that regular schools will be motivated by these schools—and by the potential loss of students—to reform. "Every state should give parents the power to choose the right public school for their children," said President Bill Clinton in his 1997 State of the Union address. "Their right to choose will foster competition and innovation that can make public schools better." That year, Congress approved $80 million to aid in the construction of new charter schools. Four years later, in 2001, there were 2,100 charter schools in the United States, including 173 charter schools run by for-profit companies. There were nearly 91,000 regular public schools.

Like other forms of school choice, charters have sparked significant debate. Chester Finn, a founding partner of Edison Schools, Inc., a private company, says, "Competition is having a salutary effect on schools and school systems as well. We are seeing examples, that are mostly anecdotal so far, of so-called regular schools responding to competition by changing their own offerings, by replenishing their faculty, by getting new textbooks, by getting a new principal or assistant principal. I think it is very important and I think it is probably going to work." Others, including historian Carl Kaestle, disagree. "I don't see any special reason, any convincing reason yet to think that competition is going to lead to better schools," Kaestle says. "Free market is not a perfect mech-

Principal leading students in the Pledge of Allegiance at the Ryder Elementary Charter School in Miami, Florida, 1999.

anism in the educational business. And I don't think the evidence so far suggests that it is." Historian James Anderson also has doubts. "Efforts at privatization and other kinds of efforts will incorporate a very small fraction of students," he says. "The vast majority of school-age students depend on a system of public education and at this point I don't see an alternative to that. And I don't even see an alternative that is of the same quality."

More than all the free-market reforms of the 1980s and 1990s, the push for high academic standards, as measured by standardized testing, has arguably had the greatest impact on classrooms nationwide. A legacy of the Reagan era, these standards and tests had bipartisan support by the end of the twentieth century. "Every state should adopt high national standards," declared President Clinton in 1997. "Every state should test every fourth-grader in reading and every eighth-grader in math to make sure these standards are met." This push for higher, measurable results has led some schools to adopt new curricula aimed at raising student achievement. Among these is the Core Knowledge curriculum, created by English professor E. D. Hirsch. It offers precisely the same academic content to students in over one thousand schools across the country, from Fort Myers, Florida, to the South Bronx, New York; from San Antonio, Texas, to Macon, Georgia. "There

The chief administrative officer poses in front of Wonderland Charter School in State College, Pennsylvania. The year 2000 marked the school's second year of operation.

A Nation at Risk?

"Core Knowledge" students in a Georgia elementary school celebrate Chinese New Year.

is no doubt that there is a core of knowledge and shared culture that the schools have an obligation to provide," Hirsch says, "for reasons not only of commonality and community but also of equity."

At Core Knowledge schools, all first-graders learn about the ancient Egyptians. All second-graders study Asian folktales and Greek myths. By the third grade, they are immersed in ancient Rome. The approach to learning is traditional and teacher-centered. All students are expected to master the same academic content at the same time. Says Georgann Reaves, "We believe that without the knowledge, without the facts, then there is no real education. You can't teach a child how to think unless you have something for him to think about."

Progressive schools, also found nationwide, offer a very different curriculum designed to enhance student achievement as well as critical thinking skills. Based on the ideas of early-twentieth-century educator John Dewey, the progressive model was put into practice in East Harlem, New York, where school choice was pioneered. In a world in which information is constantly changing, progressive schools teach children to master skills, as opposed to a set body of knowledge. "Differences of opinion are encouraged in the school, between children and grownups, between children, between children and adults," says educator Deborah Meier. "And then they are taught how you resolve differences, how to look up answers. How you find out what works and what doesn't work. So it is to create an actual little society of people who are grappling

A Nation at Risk?

with difficult ideas together." Debbie Smith, a teacher at Central Park East Secondary School, agrees. "We want to teach them how to be good thinkers. And in order to do that we have to give them the freedom to explore. My job basically is to guide them. I'm a coach, teacher as coach." Students in progressive schools learn by doing, whether writing a geometry textbook for younger students or designing and building a scale model of a house. "Projects drive our curriculum," says Smith. "Whatever the skills that we're teaching them, they always culminate in one large project so they can be proud, take ownership of something that they've done." Both progressive and Core Knowledge curricula have shown positive results in terms of student achievement and test scores.

In January 2001, President George W. Bush said, "Educational excellence for all is a national issue and at this moment is a presidential priority. Children must be tested every year. Every single year. Not just in the third grade or the eighth grade, but in the third, fourth, fifth, sixth, and seventh and eighth grades." Today, in all types of schools across the country, standardized tests and the preparation for them monopolize a growing part of the school year. Test results are posted in local newspapers, and readers know that school budgets and even property values hinge on the results. Yet even as the bar for achievement is being raised, the public education system faces tremendous challenges, from underfunding and overcrowding to school violence. More than two hundred shooting deaths occurred in American schools in the 1990s.

FACING *A young woman helps her friend with his mortarboard at their high school graduation.*

School: 1980–2000

Still, in communities throughout the United States, the vast majority of parents continue to entrust their children to public schools. "I'm not excusing problems, I'm not saying please don't evaluate public education," says journalist Nicholas Lemann. "But I think the honest starting premise has to be that on the whole public education has been a big success in America. We have more people under the roofs of public schools learning than in any of the advanced industrial democracies." In 2001, nearly 90 percent of American children—47.8 million students—were enrolled in public schools. Serving them all, and serving them well, remains an important goal. "The real object that we should be striving for in this country," says Diane Ravitch, "is to have not only a balance between excellence and equity, but a sense of their being connected. That you can't have one without the other."

For more than two hundred years, public schools have helped to make us who we are as Americans. "The public school system has been a place where literally millions of children have been able to attend, to get an education, to be influenced by dedicated teachers, who otherwise would not have had that opportunity," says James Anderson. "And so I have been critical of the development of American common schools, I have been concerned about many of the faults, many of the problems, but when all is said and done I still think that it has been fundamental to American culture. It has been a positive contribution to the development of American culture." Adds David Tyack, "I do not see any way to achieve a good future for our children more effectively than debating to-

gether and working together on how we educate that next generation. Children may be about 20 percent of the population but they
are 100 percent of the future." As Thomas Jefferson said, the future of a democracy depends on the education of its people. Today, public education is in urgent need of our support. Will we give
all students what they need to succeed, or stand by and see their
opportunities limited? That choice will determine the future of
our children—and our nation.

Acknowledgments

School, the book and the film series, is the fruit of a ten-year collaboration involving so many people from so many places and so many fields of expertise that we can only begin to thank them all. Film and television professionals, academics, and educators came together and gave generously of their talents, some for nearly a decade of their lives.

This intense collaboration is certainly due, in part, to the subject itself. Like most Americans, the members of our creative team shared a common bond of experience as former students. As parents or just plain citizens, they all had passionate opinions about public education, and thus brought a great deal of themselves to the project. It was a great privilege for us to work with Meryl Streep, whose generous spirit and amazing talent took our project to new heights.

The talented film editor Marian Hunter oversaw *School* from start to finish. Marian is a true artist. Whether she's working with scratchy black and white shots, still photographs, or vérité footage, she finds the human detail that makes a scene come alive. She is also a gifted filmmaker who harnesses her intelligence to a project, while tactfully guiding the different personalities involved. If *School* tells a good story, it's in large part thanks to Marian.

The other "storytellers" were our script writers. Terry Monmaney crystallized the original themes, beautifully bringing *School* to life in the pages of his treatments for the four episodes. Then Terry escaped to Los Angeles to pursue his career. And so, a long collaboration with a series of talented writers ensued, led by Ken Chowder, then the indomitable Joe Dorman, and Howard Weinberg (who all had to leave to work on other projects). Last came the insightful Sheila Bernard, who arrived at a "make or break" juncture, quickly got up to speed, and delivered the final scripts, followed by the book narrative. We are extremely indebted to all our writers.

Because of a tight budget, our production staff was small. Supervising producer Patty Romeu, a film scholar and a hands-on professional, was the backbone of Stone Lantern Films throughout this long project. Her good humor got us through many difficult spots. Avra Scher, associate producer, brought her consummate professionalism to the project, doing everything from troubleshooting a temperamental editing system to juggling an impossible schedule. Our highly capable friend Vera Aronow co-directed the first episode and did key research. We couldn't have finished the series or the book without their help.

The editing room is the heart and soul of any documentary film series. Ours functioned day and night thanks to a wonderful staff. Liz Renner did the hard, practical work of assembling thousands of snippets of picture, voice, and music into innumerable "rough cuts." Doug Scott, a budding director, was another essential collaborator in the cutting room. Cindy Kaplan Rooney also lent her considerable gifts as an editor to the first episode of *School*.

Of course, the editing "machine" must be fed a constant diet of interesting details and lively images. Researcher Minda Novek took on this gargantuan task, particularly for the first two shows, providing us with thousands of still pictures, engravings, paintings, and other visuals from which we tried to cull the very best. The film and book also rest on the top-notch research of Polly Pettit, Susan Milano, Deborah Snyder, and Alicia Wilson.

The music for *School* was created by two people for whom we have the utmost respect. The first is Tom Phillips, who composed more than 120 different musical pieces that fit particular scenes in the film down to the frame. This task would dissuade ordinary mortals, but Tom surprised us by accomplishing it with grace and skill. The indispensable Rena Kosersky contributed the beautiful period music that completes the film score.

Special gratitude is due to our longtime friend cinematographer Allen Moore, who is responsible for the lush look of *School* in the early episodes and much of the lively vérité footage in the later shows. Tom Hurwitz also filmed many beautifully lit interviews and scenes, as did Roger Grange. All brought taste and talent to bear on the pictures that make up the series. Cinematographer Mead Hunt, sound recordist Roger Phenix, and assistant cameraman Anthony Savini are among the technicians who deserve particular thanks as well.

The film series and the book began in 1992 as a home-grown project. We are sisters-in-law, and the idea came from Sarah Mondale's father, Clarence Mondale, an American Studies professor. At his suggestion, we set out to learn about American education, also encouraged by Sarah Mondale's mother, a teacher. In the course of our research, we contacted many experts, who in turn became consultants to the project. Stanford historian David Tyack gave constant support and guidance—the project would be nowhere without him. Many academics, including all the authors of this book, provided the intellectual framework upon which this project rests.

Still, even with the best ideas and creative talent, *School* also needed a great deal of financial help. The National Endowment for the Humanities provided essential "seed" money that allowed this project to grow. Mary Seiford of the Corporation for Public Broadcasting was an early advocate of *School,* along with Ray Bachetti of the Hewlett Foundation, Woody Wickham of the Mac-Arthur Foundation, and many other generous donors who provided financial and moral support.

Finally, Bob Lavelle, Martha Fowlkes, and the staff at Roundtable, our outreach partner, deserve a huge thank-you all their own. With their help, *School* is now being used in PTAs, boardrooms, and classrooms nationwide, providing a forum for dialogue about the past and future of public education. This was our dream ten years ago, and we can't believe that now, thanks in large part to the great folks at Roundtable, we seem close to achieving it. This was also the dream of David Crippens of KCET (PBS-Los Angeles) when he first decided to take on this project. His advice and encouragement proved more valuable than

Acknowledgments

he knows. Joyce Campbell, Mare Mazur, and Laurel Lambert of KCET also deserve special recognition.

School, the film as well as the book, was nourished by a host of collaborators who gave their best to the project. We thank Deb Chasman and Julie Hassel at Beacon Press for making this book a reality and for their hard work under such a pressing deadline. To those mentioned here, and to those who are not included here, we extend our deepest thanks.

SARAH MONDALE AND SARAH PATTON

Acknowledgments

BIBLIOGRAPHY

Anderson, James D. *The Education of Blacks in the South, 1860–1935*. Chapel Hill: University of North Carolina Press, 1988.

Bailyn, Bernard. *Education in the Forming of American Society*. Chapel Hill: University of North Carolina Press, 1960.

Beals, Melba Pattillo. *Warriors Don't Cry: A Searing Memoir of the Battle to Integrate Little Rock's Central High*. New York: Pocket Books, 1994.

Bond, Horace Mann. *The Education of the Negro in the American Social Order*. 1934. Reprint, New York: Octagon Books, 1966.

Brumberg, Stephan F. *Going to America, Going to School: The Jewish Immigrant Public School Encounter in Turn-of-the-Century New York City*. New York: Praeger Publishers, 1986.

Chapman, Paul Davis. *Schools as Sorters: Lewis M. Terman, Applied Psychology, and the Intelligence Testing Movement, 1890–1930*. New York: New York University Press, 1988.

Chubb, John E., and Terry M. Moe. *Politics, Markets & America's Schools*. Washington, DC: The Brookings Institution, 1991.

Cohen, Ronald D. *Children of the Mill: Schooling and Society in Gary, Indiana, 1906–1960*. Bloomington, IN: Indiana University Press, 1990.

Cornelius, Janet Duitsman. *When I Can Read My Title Clear: Literacy, Slavery, and Religion in the Antebellum South*. Columbia: University of South Carolina Press, 1991.

Cremin, Lawrence A. *The American Common School*. New York: Teachers College, Columbia University, 1951.

———. *American Education: The Colonial Experience, 1607–1783*. New York: Harper & Row, 1970.

———. *American Education: The Metropolitan Experience, 1876–1980*. New York: Harper & Row, 1988.

———. *American Education: The National Experience, 1783–1876*. New York: Harper & Row, 1980.

———. *Popular Education and Its Discontents*. New York: Harper & Row, 1990.

———. *Traditions of American Education*. New York: Basic Books, Inc., 1977.

———. *The Transformation of the School*. New York: Alfred A. Knopf, 1969.

Cuban, Larry. *How Teachers Taught: Constancy and Change in American Classrooms, 1890–1980*. New York: Teachers College Press, 1993.

Cubberley, Ellwood P. *Public Education in the United States*. Boston: Houghton, Mifflin Company, 1919.

Curry, Constance. *Silver Rights*. Chapel Hill: Algonquin Books, 1995.

Fass, Paula. *Outside In: Minorities and the Transformation of American Education*. New York: Oxford University Press, 1989.

Gonzalez, Gilbert. *Chicano Education in the Era of Segregation*. Philadelphia: Balch Institute Press, 1990.

Hale, Grace Elizabeth. *Making Whiteness: The Culture of Segregation in the South, 1890–1940*. New York: Pantheon Books, 1998.

Horton, James Oliver, and Lois E. Horton. *Black Bostonians*. New York: Holmes and Meier Publishers, Inc., 1979.

Johnson, Clifton. *Old Time Schools and Schoolbooks*. Dover, 1963.

Kaestle, Carl F. *The Pillars of the Republic: Common Schools and American Society, 1780–1860*. New York: Hill & Wang, 1983.

Kaestle, Carl F. and Helen Damon-Moore. *Literacy in the United States: Readers and Reading Since 1880*. New Haven: Yale University Press, 1991.

Kantor, Harvey, and David Tyack, eds. *Work, Youth, and Schooling: Historical Perspectives on Vocationalism in American Education*. Stanford, CA: Stanford University Press, 1982.

Karier, Clarence J., Paul Violas, and Joel Spring. *Roots of Crisis: American Education in the Twentieth Century*. Chicago: Rand McNally, 1973.

Katz, Michael B. *Class, Bureaucracy and American Schools*. New York: Praeger Publishers, 1973.

———. *The Irony of Early School Reform: Educational Innovation in Mid-Nineteenth Century Massachusetts*. Cambridge, MA: Harvard University Press, 1968.

———. *Reconstructing American Education*. Cambridge, MA: Harvard University Press, 1987.

Katznelson, Ira, and Margaret Weir. *Schooling for All: Class, Race and the Decline of the Democratic Ideal*. New York: Basic Books, 1985.

Kliebard, Herbert. *Schooled to Work: Vocationalism and the American Curriculum, 1876–1946*. New York: Teachers College Press, 1999.

Kluger, Richard. *Simple Justice*. New York: Alfred A. Knopf, 1975.

Lazerson, Marvin, and W. Norton Grubb, eds. *American Education and Vocationalism*. New York: Teachers College Press, 1974.

Levin, H. "Educational Performance Standards and the Economy." *Educational Researcher* 27(4): 4–10 (1998).

Meier, Deborah. *The Power of Their Ideas: Lessons for America from a Small School in Harlem*. Boston: Beacon Press, 1995.

Messerli, Jonathan. *Horace Mann*. New York: Alfred A. Knopf, 1971.

Nietz, John A. *Old Textbooks*. Pittsburgh: University of Pittsburgh Press, 1961.

Perlman, Joel. *Ethnic Difference*. Cambridge: Cambridge University Press, 1988.

Ravitch, Diane. *The Great School Wars: A History of the New York City Public Schools*. New York: Basic Books, 1988.

———. *The Revisionists Revisited: A Critique on the Radical Attack on Schools*. New York: Basic Books, 1978.

———. *The Troubled Crusade: American Education, 1945–1980*. New York: Basic Books, 1983.

San Miguel, Guadalupe. *"Let All of Them Take Heed": Mexican Americans and the Campaign for Educational Equality in Texas, 1910–1981*. Austin: University of Texas Press, 1987.

Sears, Jesse B. and Adin D. Henderson. *Cubberley of Stanford and His Contribution to American Education*. Stanford: Stanford University Press, 1957.

Shipps, Dorothy. "Echoes of Corporate Influence." In *Reconstructing The Common Good in Education: Coping with Intractable American Dilemmas,* edited by Larry Cuban and Dorothy Shipps, 82–106. Stanford, CA: Stanford University Press, 2000.

Sklar, Kathryn Kish. *Catharine Beecher: A Study in American Domesticity*. New Haven: Yale University Press, 1973.

Spring, Joel H. *The American School 1642–1996*. New York: McGraw Hill Companies, Inc., 1997.

———. *Education and the Rise of the Corporate State*. Boston: Beacon Press, 1972.

———. *The Sorting Machine: National Educational Policy Since 1945*. New York: The David McKay Company, Inc., 1976.

Tyack, David B. *The One Best System: A History of American Urban Education*. Cambridge, MA: Harvard University Press, 1974.

Tyack, David B., and Larry Cuban. *Tinkering Toward Utopia: A Century of Public School Reform*. Cambridge, MA: Harvard University Press, 1995.

Tyack, David B. and Elisabeth Hansot. *Learning Together: A History of Coeducation in American Public Schools*. New Haven: Yale University Press, 1990.

Tyack, David B. and Elisabeth Hansot. *Managers of Virtue: Public School Leadership in America 1820–1980*. New York: Basic Books, 1982.

Weiss, Bernard J., ed. *American Education and the European Immigrant, 1840–1940*. Urbana: University of Illinois Press, 1982.

Welts Kaufman, Polly. *Women Teachers on the Frontier*. New Haven: Yale University Press, 1984.

White, Richard. *Remembering Ahanagran: Storytelling in a Family's Past*. New York: Hill & Wang, 1998.

ABOUT THE AUTHORS

JAMES D. ANDERSON is professor and head of the Department of Educational Policy Studies and professor of history at the University of Illinois at Urbana-Champaign. He is author of *The Education of Blacks in the South, 1860–1935* (University of North Carolina Press, 1988).

SHEILA CURRAN BERNARD is an Emmy Award–winning filmmaker whose credits include the PBS series *Eyes on the Prize, I'll Make Me a World,* and *America's War on Poverty.* She has been a fellow at the McDowell Colony and the Virginia Center for the Creative Arts.

LARRY CUBAN, a former high school social studies teacher and school superintendent, is professor of education at Stanford University. He has written extensively on school reform, teaching, leadership, and the uses of technology in schools. *Oversold and Underused: Computers in Schools* will be published by Harvard University Press in 2001.

CARL F. KAESTLE is University Professor and Professor of Education, History, and Public Policy at Brown University. Among his books are *Pillars of the Republic: Common Schools and American Society, 1780–1860* (Hill & Wang, 1983) and *Literacy in the United States: Readers and Reading Since 1880* (Yale University Press, 1991).

SARAH MONDALE, director and co-producer of the television series *School,* has directed and co-produced the award-winning PBS documentary films *Marcel Proust: A Writer's Life* and *Asylum,* which earned her an Emmy nomination. She also wrote, directed, and produced the 35mm short film *Old Acquaintances* (HBO/Cinemax). Ms. Mondale is co-chair of Stone Lantern Films, Inc., and lives in the New York area.

DIANE RAVITCH holds the Brown Chair in Education Studies at the Brookings Institution and is a research professor at NYU. She has written or edited seventeen books, the latest of which is *Left Back: A Century of Failed School Reforms* (Simon & Schuster, 2000).

DAVID TYACK is the Vida Jacks Professor of Education and professor emeritus of history at Stanford University. He is the author of, among other books, *The One Best System: A History of American Education* (Harvard University Press, 1974) and co-author, with Larry Cuban, of *Tinkering Toward Utopia: A Century of Public School Reform* (Harvard University Press, 1995).

INDEX

Note: Page numbers in *italics* indicate illustrations.

Index

core knowledge. *See* curriculum, Core
Knowledge

corporations, as model for school administration, 178, 179

criticism: of busing, 129, 167; of charter
schools, 205; of the Gary Plan, 68,
91–93; of I.Q. testing, 67, 103–4; of life
adjustment education, 114–15; of privatization, 202, 203; of public education, 2, 16–17, 69, 177

Crystal City High School, Texas, 150–57;
strike by students in, 127, 132–34,
152–53, 155, *155*

Cuban, Larry, 77, 115, 117

Cubberley, Ellwood P., 97–98, *98*

culture, public, 126, 212–13

curriculum: academic, *99*, 190, 192, 194;
colonial, 21; commercialization of, 179;
Core Knowledge, 207–209; debate
about, 64; demands for more rigorous,
69, 115, 127–28, 177–78, 181, 187;
diversification of, as "progressive," 67,
86, 113–15; early twentieth-century,
64; effect of *Sputnik* on, 119; failings
of, 28; federal funding for science and
languages in, 69; immigrants' demands
and, 92–93; late nineteenth-century,
58; local control over, 129; reform of,
76–77, 180; religious studies in, 3, 96,
127; tracking and. *See* tracking; vocationalized, 180–81

Dandridge, Irene, 200, 202, 203

debates, on schooling, in New York, 34, 36

decentralization, of education, 4

Delaine, Joseph Albert, 124

democracy: cultural, 8; economic, 8;
importance of education for, 2, 13, 23,
25, 63, 184, 213; redefining, in urban
society, 6–7

demographics, change in, and integration, 168

Depression, the Great, and school attendance, 103

desegregation. *See* integration

Detroit: busing in, 165–67; schools in,
127, *166*

Dewey, John, 2, 8, 67, 76–77, *77*, 78, 114,
115, 209

disabilities, equal opportunity and, 128;
lack of, 133; politics and, 8; privatization and, 202; schooling for children
with, 65, 162–63

discrimination. *See* education, discriminatory practices in

disease, in public schools, 76, *87*

diversity: among students, 91, 94; and
control of education, 130

domestic science. *See* home economics

Douglass, Frederick, 41

Doyle, Greg, 194, 195

Drew High School, Mississippi, 125

EAI. *See* Education Alternatives, Inc.

East Harlem school district, reform in,
187–90, 204, 209

economy, the, and education, 12, 14,
148–58, 174–75, 177, 186–87

Edison Schools, Inc., 205

education: adult, 65; bilingual, 127, 128,
157–59; as a business, 202; child-
centered, 67, 78, 86; in the colonies,
11–13, 20–22, 23; as a common good, 2,
4, 8, 29, 182; compulsory, 76, 103; as a
consumer good, 8, 182; costs of, 178;
discriminatory practices in, 163, 165,

198–99; distrust of public, 4; equality in. *See* equality; excellence in. *See* excellence, academic; immigrants' attitudes toward, 65, 96–97; importance of, 1–2, 13, 149–58; industrial. *See* education, vocational; "life adjustment," 68–69, 113–15; politics of, 8; progressive, 67, 76–77, 86–91, 175, 180–81; as a public obligation, 30; purpose of, 5, *20*, 22–23, 25, 41, 130, 149–50, 158–59, 174, 184, 212; quality of, 28, 29–30; "separate but equal" doctrine in, 45, 134, 135, 137, 138, 161; and the separation of church and state, 36, 194–98; standardizing, 7; technical. *See* education, vocational; universal, 23, 64, 68, 70; vocational, 65–66, 67, 68, *80*, 107, *110*, 162, 174–75, 176, 180

Education Alternatives, Inc. (EAI), 187, 201, 203–204

Educational Wastelands (Bestor), 69, 115

Edwards, Marie, 83, 85, 89

efficiency: bureaucratization and, 97–98, 176; tracking and, 66, 98–99

Eisenhower, Dwight, 119, 125, 143

elementary school, enrollment in, 63–64

Emerson School, *50*, *82*

English: for instruction, 73, 93, 94, 95, 112, 150–52, 158; for I.Q. tests, 103–4

enrollment, 4, 184; in college, 132, 159; in elementary school, 63–64; in high school, 64, 97, 126; in integrated schools, 144, 149; in public schools, 58, 73, 212

equality: academic excellence and, 128; expectations for, 29, 120, 132; federal funding and, 146; movement for, 41–46, 134, 146

equipment, *57*, 201

Erstes Lesebuch (First Reader), *91*

Essex Street Market School, *74*

ethnicity, intelligence and, 101

excellence, academic: as a casualty of equality, 128; corporate models for, 178; demands for, 127–28, 129; and equal opportunity, 128–29

exercise, in school, 77, *80*

expenditure, on boys' sports, 161; on public schools, 58. *See also* financing

experts. *See* professionalization

facilities: black schools, 42; early twentieth-century, 75–76, *87;* federal funding for, 205; frontier schools, *47*, *48*, *54*; in Gary, Indiana, 78, 85, 86; neglect of, 68; nineteenth-century, 28–29, *29*, *78–80*, *82;* privatization and, *200*, 201

Faubus, Orville, 142, 143

field trips, *81*, *83*

financing, as a civic obligation, 20; for education, 11, 15–16, 27, 30, 64, 97, 174, 202; federal, 69, 119, 128, 146, 148, 158, 161, 175, 205; inequalities in, 137, 155, 161, 165, 187, 196; local control of, 203; magnet schools and, 190, 192; privatized administration and, 201; for vouchers, 193, 194. *See also* expenditure; vouchers

Finn, Chester, 20, 97, 119, 168, 193, 196, 205

First World War, effect of, on immigrants, 95

Fleming School, Detroit, *166*

Flesch, Rudolph, 69

Fliegel, Seymour, 188, 189, 204

Florida, school in, *201*

Fordham University, 162

core knowledge. *See* curriculum, Core Knowledge

corporations, as model for school administration, 178, 179

criticism: of busing, 129, 167; of charter schools, 205; of the Gary Plan, 68, 91–93; of I.Q. testing, 67, 103–4; of life adjustment education, 114–15; of privatization, 202, 203; of public education, 2, 16–17, 69, 177

Crystal City High School, Texas, 150–57; strike by students in, 127, 132–34, 152–53, 155, *155*

Cuban, Larry, 77, 115, 117

Cubberley, Ellwood P., 97–98, *98*

culture, public, 126, 212–13

curriculum: academic, *99*, 190, 192, 194; colonial, 21; commercialization of, 179; Core Knowledge, 207–209; debate about, 64; demands for more rigorous, 69, 115, 127–28, 177–78, 181, 187; diversification of, as "progressive," 67, 86, 113–15; early twentieth-century, 64; effect of *Sputnik* on, 119; failings of, 28; federal funding for science and languages in, 69; immigrants' demands and, 92–93; late nineteenth-century, 58; local control over, 129; reform of, 76–77, 180; religious studies in, 3, 96, 127; tracking and. *See* tracking; vocationalized, 180–81

Dandridge, Irene, 200, 202, 203

debates, on schooling, in New York, 34, 36

decentralization, of education, 4

Delaine, Joseph Albert, 124

democracy: cultural, 8; economic, 8; importance of education for, 2, 13, 23, 25, 63, 184, 213; redefining, in urban society, 6–7

demographics, change in, and integration, 168

Depression, the Great, and school attendance, 103

desegregation. *See* integration

Detroit: busing in, 165–67; schools in, 127, *166*

Dewey, John, 2, 8, 67, 76–77, *77*, 78, 114, 115, 209

disabilities, equal opportunity and, 128; lack of, 133; politics and, 8; privatization and, 202; schooling for children with, 65, 162–63

discrimination. *See* education, discriminatory practices in

disease, in public schools, 76, *87*

diversity: among students, 91, 94; and control of education, 130

domestic science. *See* home economics

Douglass, Frederick, 41

Doyle, Greg, 194, 195

Drew High School, Mississippi, 125

EAI. *See* Education Alternatives, Inc.

East Harlem school district, reform in, 187–90, 204, 209

economy, the, and education, 12, 14, 148–58, 174–75, 177, 186–87

Edison Schools, Inc., 205

education: adult, 65; bilingual, 127, 128, 157–59; as a business, 202; child-centered, 67, 78, 86; in the colonies, 11–13, 20–22, 23; as a common good, 2, 4, 8, 29, 182; compulsory, 76, 103; as a consumer good, 8, 182; costs of, 178; discriminatory practices in, 163, 165,

Index

Index

Index

Index

PHOTO CREDITS

19 Courtesy of Sotheby's, Inc.

20 Northern Illinois University, College of Education, Blackwell History of Education Museum.

20 Portrait of schoolmaster reading to two boys. Colonial Williamsburg Foundation Abby Aldrich Rockefeller Folk Art Museum, Williamsburg, Virginia.

21 Library of Congress.

23 Independence National Historical Park Collection, National Park Service.

24 Terra Foundation for the Arts, Daniel J. Terra Collection, 1992.122; photograph courtesy of Terra Foundation for the Arts, Chicago.

26 Library of Congress. Produced by Mathew Brady Studio.

27 Northern Illinois University, College of Education, Blackwell History of Education Museum.

28 Library of Congress.

29 Northern Illinois University, College of Education, Blackwell History of Education Museum.

30 The DeWitt Historical Society of Tompkins County, Ithaca, New York.

32 Library of Congress.

33 Library of Congress.

34 Library of Congress. Engraved by J. H. Forrest from a photograph by Mathew Brady.

35 Robert Dennis Collection of Stereoscopic Views. Photography Collection. Miriam and Ira D. Wallach Division of Arts, Prints, and Photographs. The New York Public Library.

37 Library of Congress.

38 From "A Full and Complete Account of the Late Awful Riots in Philadelphia." The Library Company of Philadelphia.

39 Robert Dennis Collection of Stereoscopic Views. Photography Collection. Miriam and Ira D. Wallach Division of Art, Prints, and Photographs. The New York Public Library.

40 With permission of Crabtree Publishing.

40 The New-York Historical Society.

41 Boston Athenaeum.

43 Nebraska State Historical Society.

45 Photographs and Prints Division. Schomburg Center for Research in Black Culture, The New York Public Library, Astor, Lenox, and Tilden Foundations.

46 Northern Illinois University, College of Education, Blackwell History of Education Museum.

47 Library of Congress.

48 National Archives.

48 State Historical Society of North Dakota.

49 The Schlesinger Library, Radcliffe Institute, Harvard University.

50 The Metropolitan Museum of Art, Gift of I. N. Phelps Stokes, Edward S. Hawes, Alice Mary Hawes, and Marion Augusta Hawes.

51 Library of Congress.

51 Indiana Historical Society.

52 Montana Historical Society, Helena, Montana

53 Northern Illinois University, College of Education, Blackwell History of Education Museum.

54 The DeWitt Historical Society of Tompkins County, Ithaca, New York. Verne Morton Photograph Collection.

55 Nebraska State Historical Society.

56 The DeWitt Historical Society of Tompkins County, Ithaca, New York. Verne Morton Photograph Collection.

56 Photograph by George Barker. Library of Congress.

57 From *The School and the Schoolmaster,* by Alonzo Potter and George B. Emerson.

57 From *Common School Journal,* ca. 1840s.

59 Sheldon Jackson Collections. Princeton Collections of Western Americana. Princeton University Library.

59 Photograph by Salter.

60 Photograph by John N. Choate (1848–1902). Sheldon Jackson Collections. Princeton Collections of Western Americana. Princeton University Library.

60 George Edward Anderson Collection, L. Tom Perry Special Collections Library, Brigham Young University, Provo, Utah.

71 Library of Congress.

72 American Jewish Joint Distribution Committee Photo Archives.

73 Museum of the City of New York. The Jacob A. Riis Collection.

74 Museum of the City of New York. The Jacob A. Riis Collection.

74 Museum of the City of New York. The Jacob A. Riis Collection.

75 Museum of the City of New York. The Jacob A. Riis Collection.

75 The DeWitt Historical Society of Tompkins County, Ithaca, New York. Verne Morton Photograph Collection.

76 Library of Congress.

77 Library of Congress.

77 Lander MacClintock Photo Collection, Special Collections, Morris Library, Southern Illinois University, Carbondale, Illinois.

78 Library of Congress. Photograph by Frances Benjamin Johnston.

79 Library of Congress. Photograph by Frances Benjamin Johnston.

79 Library of Congress. Photograph by Frances Benjamin Johnston.

80 Library of Congress. Photograph by Frances Benjamin Johnston.

80 Library of Congress. Photograph by Frances Benjamin Johnston.

81 Library of Congress. Photograph by Frances Benjamin Johnston.

82 Library of Congress. Photograph by Frances Benjamin Johnston.

82 Library of Congress. Photograph by Frances Benjamin Johnston.

83 Calumet Regional Archives, Indiana University Northwest.

84 Calumet Regional Archives, Indiana University Northwest.

85 Calumet Regional Archives, Indiana University Northwest.

86 Bain Collection, Library of Congress.

87 New York City Board of Education Archives, Milbank Memorial Library, Teachers College, Columbia University.

87 Museum of the City of New York. The Jacob A. Riis Collection.

88 New York City Board of Education Archives, Milbank Memorial Library, Teachers College, Columbia University.

89 Calumet Regional Archives, Indiana University Northwest.

90 Northern Illinois University, College of Education, Blackwell History of Education Museum.

91 Indiana University Purdue University Indianapolis. IUPUI University Library, Special Collections and Archives.

92 Minnesota Historical Society.

93 Miriam and Ira D. Wallach Division of Art, Prints and Photographs. The New York Public Library.

94 Museum of the City of New York. The Jacob A. Riis Collection.

95 Courtesy of Bel Kaufman.

98 Department of Special Collections, Stanford University Libraries.

98 Department of Special Collections, Stanford University Libraries.

99 Library of Congress. Photograph by Frances Benjamin Johnston.

100 Special Collections, Milbank Memorial Library, Teachers College, Columbia University.

101 From *A Study of American Intelligence* by Carl C. Brigham (Princeton: Princeton University Press, 1923).

105 George I. Sanchez Papers, Nettie Lee Benson Latin American Collection. The University of Texas at Austin.

106 Los Angeles Unified School District.

108 Courtesy of the Nava family.

110 Los Angeles Unified School District.

111 Corbis.

114 Library of Congress.

116 TimePix.

117 Published by The National Council for American Education. New York Public Library.

131 Photo by Carl Iwasaki/TimePix

132 Topeka Public Schools Communications Department.

133 Topeka Public Schools Communications Department.

134 Topeka Public Schools Communications Department.

136 Library of Congress.

137 Kansas Collection, Spencer Research Library, Kansas State University.

139 Photograph by Carl Iwasaki/TimePix.

140 Corbis.

Photo Credits

Photo Credits

Photo Credits

FILM CREDITS

School: The Story of American Public Education

DIRECTOR
Sarah Mondale

CO-PRODUCERS
Sarah Patton and Sarah Mondale

NARRATOR
Meryl Streep

EDITOR
Marian Sears Hunter

WRITER
Sheila Curran Bernard

ORIGINAL MUSIC
Tom Phillips

SUPERVISING PRODUCER
Patricia Romeu

ASSOCIATE PRODUCER
Avra Scher

CO-DIRECTOR, EPISODE 1
Vera Aronow

CINEMATOGRAPHY
Allen Moore
Tom Hurwitz
Roger T. Grange, III
Mead Hunt

ACADEMIC CONSULTANTS
David B. Tyack
Carl E. Kaestle
Jeffrey Mirel
James D. Anderson
William J. Reese
Michael B. Katz
Thomas Bender
Michael W. Sedlak
Lynn D. Gordon
Vincent P. Franklin
Kathryn Kish Sklar
Clarence C. Mondale
Guadalupe San Miguel
Gilbert G. Gonzalez
Stephan F. Brumberg

ORIGINAL TREATMENT
Terence Monmaney

ADDITIONAL WRITING
Ken Chowder
Joseph Dorman
Howard Weinberg

DIRECTOR OF RESEARCH, EPISODE 1
Minda Novek

MUSIC SUPERVISOR
Rena C. Kosersky

SERIES ASSOCIATE EDITOR
Elizabeth Renner

ADDITIONAL EDITING
Cindy Kaplan Rooney

ASSOCIATE EDITOR
Douglas Scott

PHOTO ANIMATION PHOTOGRAPHY
Gary Becker

PRODUCTION COORDINATOR
Neil Landau

SOUND
Roger Phenix
Mark Roy
John Bucher
Richard Fleming
Steve Lafayette
Peter Miller
John Osborne
Len Schmitz
Bob Silverthorne
Ken King
John Haptas
Michael Lonsdale
Mark Lutte
John Eagin
Matt Quast
J. C. Schlageter
David Terry
Dennis Townsend

Film Credits

Dr. Vance Grant
Donald Scott
Tad Thompson
Lucy Castillo
Dennis Bixler Marquez
Bradley Stauffer
Greg Doyle
Virginia Mondale
Walter F. Mondale
Rachel Franklin-Weekley
Katie Roy
John Cronin
Emily Sklar
The Kazin Family
Billie Gammon

WE WOULD LIKE TO THANK THE FOLLOWING
SCHOOLS FOR ALLOWING US TO FILM:
Miller Middle School, Macon, GA
Cale Elementary School, Charlottesville, VA
Urban Peace Academy, New York, NY
Sumner School, Topeka, KS
Harambee School, Milwaukee, WI
Urban Day School, Milwaukee, WI
Elm Creative Arts, Milwaukee, WI
Crystal City Schools, Crystal City, TX
Horace Mann School, Gary, IN
Froebel School, Gary, IN
Upper Nyack School, Nyack, NY
Phillips School, Boston, MA
Smith School, Boston, MA
Massapequa High School, Massapequa, NY
Montclair High School, Montclair, NJ
Central Park East Secondary School,
New York, NY
Harlem Park Community School, Baltimore, MD
P.S. 166, New York, NY
Topeka High School, Topeka, KS
Roosevelt High School, Los Angeles, CA
Bellagio Newcomer School, Los Angeles, CA

PUBLIC ENGAGEMENT CAMPAIGN PRODUCED BY
Roundtable, Inc.

EXECUTIVE IN CHARGE
FOR KCET/HOLLYWOOD
Mare Mazur

COORDINATING PRODUCER
FOR KCET/HOLLYWOOD
Joyce Campbell

KCET/HOLLYWOOD EXECUTIVE
IN CHARGE FOR OUTREACH
David Crippens

Funding Provided by
CORPORATION FOR PUBLIC BROADCASTING
NATIONAL ENDOWMENT FOR THE HUMANITIES
THE JOHN D. AND CATHERINE T.
MACARTHUR FOUNDATION
THE WILLIAM AND FLORA
HEWLETT FOUNDATION
CARNEGIE CORPORATION OF NEW YORK
THE FORD FOUNDATION
LOVELACE FAMILY TRUST
THE ANNENBERG FOUNDATION
THE ARTHUR VINING DAVIS FOUNDATIONS
THE EDNA MCCONNELL CLARK FOUNDATION
THE NEW YORK COMMUNITY TRUST
THE SPENCER FOUNDATION
THE GEORGE GUND FOUNDATION
THE WILLIAM H. DONNER FOUNDATION
HILLSDALE FUND
JOHN S. AND JAMES L. KNIGHT FOUNDATION
METLIFE FOUNDATION
W.K. KELLOGG FOUNDATION
THE JAMES FORD BELL FOUNDATION
NEW YORK COUNCIL FOR THE HUMANITIES
THE PAUL ROBESON FUND FOR
INDEPENDENT MEDIA/FUNDING EXCHANGE

Film Credits